LOVE DHARMA

LOVE DHARMA

Relationship Wisdom from
Enlightened Buddhist Women

Geri Larkin

JOURNEY EDITIONS
Boston • Tokyo • Singapore

First published in 2003 by Journey Editions, an imprint of Periplus Editions (HK) Ltd., with editorial offices at 153 Milk Street, Boston, Massachusetts 02109.

Library of Congress Cataloging-in-Publication Data
Larkin, Geraldine A.
  Love dharma: relationship wisdom from enlightened Buddhist women /
Geri Larkin. — 1st ed.
    p. cm.
Includes bibliographical references.
  ISBN 1-58290-063-9 (pbk.)
  1. Man-woman relationships. 2. Man-woman relationships—Religious
aspects—Buddhism. 3. Marriage—Religious aspects—Buddhism. 4.
Women—Conduct of life. 5. Buddhist women—Conduct of
life—History—Case studies. I. Title.
  HQ801 .L2984 2002
  306.7—dc 21
                                2002073011

Distributed by:
NORTH AMERICA, LATIN AMERICA, AND EUROPE
Tuttle Publishing
Distribution Center
Airport Industrial Park
364 Innovation Drive
North Clarendon, VT 05759-9436
Tel: (802) 773-8930 Tel: (800) 526-2778 Fax: (802) 773-6993

JAPAN AND KOREA
Tuttle Publishing
Yaekari Bldg., 3F
5-4-12 Ōsaki, Shinagawa-ku
Tokyo 141-0032
Tel: 81-35-437-0171 Fax: 81-35-437-0755

ASIA PACIFIC
Berkeley Books Pte. Ltd.
130 Joo Seng Road
#06-01/03 Olivine Building
Singapore 368357
Tel: (65) 6280-1330 Fax: (65) 6280-6290

First edition
05 04 03   9 8 7 6 5 4 3 2 1

Design by Victor Mingovits
Printed in the United States of America

A DISCLAIMER

I want to say this early in the book. If you are in an abusive relationship—your partner hits, shoves, verbally abuses you; your partner drinks too much, takes recreational drugs, gambles, or reads/watches pornography regularly—leave it. Get out. By staying in an abusive relationship you are feeding the most negative karma possible, both for you and your abusive partner, because you are locking yourself into a situation of anger and fear (both huge impediments to enlightenment—on the chance that you need some added incentive) and locking your abuser into a horrific future once the karmic payback kicks in. Get help. There are too many domestic violence and sexual assault centers in place—at least in the United States—for you to pretend you can't.

This book is dedicated to all women.
You know who you are.

CONTENTS

ACKNOWLEDGMENTS

Thank-yous to: Andrea Pedolsky, who encouraged me to write this book. Jennifer Lantagne, who had the courage to edit it. The Still Point sangha, and especially to Koho Vince Anila, who, when I said I vowed to become fully enlightened in a female form, said, "Me, too."

I bow to the ground in gratitude.

INTRODUCTION

The gross bodies of men and women are equally suited,
But if a woman has strong aspiration, she has higher
potential.
From beginningless time you have accrued merit from
virtue and awareness,
And now, faultless, endowed with a Buddha's Qualities,
Superior woman, you are a human Bodhisattva.
This is you I am speaking of, happy girl, is it not?
Now that you have achieved your own enlightenment,
Work for others, for the sake of other beings.

—VICKI MACKENZIE, *Cave in the Snow*

To SAY THAT THE ANCIENT women who lived during the
time of the Buddha 2,500 years ago had difficult lives may be
the understatement of several millennia. Tucked into plains
shadowed by the mountains of Nepal, each woman lived with
the three seasons of desert heat, downpours, and bone-chilling
cold year after year. They depended utterly on the harvests of
local farms for food and on the goodwill of spouses and
extended families for shelter. They lost their babies, their children, their lovers, their beauty, their youth, and sometimes
their hope.

What's amazing about their stories, long hidden from
Western eyes, is how familiar they are. Their struggles, their

heartbreaks, are ours. Abandonment, affairs, loneliness, and jealousy—these women lived through all of them. Capa, a beautiful young woman, daughter of a trapper, lost her heart to a young monk. Deeply in love with him, she survived his abandonment of her with a spunkiness that would make any woman proud. Plus, she realized that not only could she live without him, but she could use his leaving as a springboard for her own spiritual work. Patacara watched her two small children die before her very eyes on the same day she lost her husband and her parents. The wildness of her despair even moved the Buddha. She learned what it meant to dig deep within herself to find solace. And she learned that what she needed to go on living was already within her heart. Queen Mallika would have blowout battles with her husband, while Magandiya was so overtaken with jealousy that she killed her husband's lover. Pajapati, already brokenhearted that her son deserted their royal family in search of enlightenment, faced ongoing hardships as her community, abandoned, sank into poverty and ultimately warred with neighboring kingdoms. Out of her despair grew a determination to deepen her own spiritual practice so she could be helpful to other women suffering the same losses.

Each of these women did more than survive. They are remembered in Buddhist texts because they were able to transform the tragedies of their lives into their own deep experience of enlightenment. There is an old Buddhist saying: If you meet the tiger in the jungle and he opens his mouth to eat you, you must put your head all the way into his mouth. That's exactly what these ancient women did. In embracing the truth of their situations and not running from their emotions, by allowing despair to surface and provide grist for their spiritual work, each woman was transformed. Today we would call them saints.

A new millennium is an auspicious time to rediscover the wisdom of the ancients. Their stories have been hidden for too long. It's not just that the female followers of Buddha have been less exposed to us—although that is true—it's that things have been tougher for women in this tradition. As a result, their stories are fewer and farther between, so the energy we could draw from them has been largely left untapped. Okay, there's Tara in the Tibetan tradition and Kuan Yin, the bod-hisattva of compassion in Zen, but for every Tara and Kuan Yin we've heard of handfuls of male Milarepas and Dalai Lamas and masters like Dogen and Hakuin and Chinul.

What a loss.

And yet what a joy to find again life stories that offer up the truth of everyday enlightenment and different perspectives on how to heal heartbreak. If these women could suffer the inevitable hardships life brings, transform their difficulties into a search for their own wisdom hearts, so can we—whether we are working mothers, working fathers, housewives, househus-bands, single, not single, or sort of single. Not only do these women provide inspiration, they also prove the universality of enlightenment. It's one thing to be a prince who decides to dedicate his life to spiritual seeking. It's another to be an old woman, rejected by your entire extended family, who manages to discover the path to happiness not just in spite of it all but by using it all. That's why it is the experience of women, not men, that is so significant in these times of relationship confu-sion writ large.

Let's face it: Times are tough. The speed of change has made most of our lives chaotic. Issues have become more complex. It's a good time to clear up and hunker down. A new century offers the perfect opportunity for embracing a different approach to living—one that is direct, open, compassionate, and wise. It offers us an opportunity to try out alternative ways, maybe even ancient ones, of responding to our world.

Not that I'm pointing any fingers, but you and I could still be stuck in the rut of reacting to difficult situations in the same way. A lover leaves and we obsess about getting even. The new wife is nasty and we're drawn to doing what we can to make her life miserable. The community we live in is fraying around the edges, yet we don't even know the names of our neighbors. Lowering crime statistics notwithstanding, we dash from car to home each night, battening down our physical and psychological hatches until the morning comes and we get back into the fray. Loneliness has taken over many of our days, while we continue to lose whole decades in the blink of an eye.

Let's try looking backward for some emotional and spiritual help. Twenty-five hundred years ago the Buddha offered up some powerful teachings on how we could climb our way out of our unhappiness. His four noble truths—that life brings with it suffering, that we suffer because we are always wanting something more, that there is a path out of suffering, and that path consists of deep morality mixed with a bare attention to our lives—have become the centerpiece for a formula followed by millions of spiritual seekers, starting with the ancients, wanting to find the place of deep contentment and joy that we are actually beginning to believe is our birthright.

Ancient Buddhist women have shown us that by sinking our teeth into our spiritual practice, we allow to surface an abiding wisdom that can help us survive the worst possible personal tragedies. This wisdom, this crazy wisdom, as often as not contradicts conventional wisdom, offering whole new possibilities for approaching the gunk of our lives. Crazy wisdom is literally a form a wisdom that seems crazy at first but, through the lens of time, proves to be exactly right for the situation. It can seed unimagined solutions to problems that have made us writhe in pain for years. It can create community as we begin to actually talk to each other and hear the words and feelings coming out of our mouths. It offers up the possibility of peace and a world held precious by its inhabitants. Finally, at its most ripe, crazy wisdom is the complete manifestation of the four perfections—equanimity, joy, compassion, and loving kindness—the elements of our own enlightenment.

Love Dharma is a collection of stories that illustrate the impact crazy wisdom has on people's lives. These stories of the early female followers of the Buddha, women who have been largely unknown outside Buddhist academic circles, make up the heart of this book. Each woman had to lean into her own crazy wisdom to survive and eventually discover her own enlightened heart. For each chapter, I have pulled the theme of each woman's story forward to this century to demonstrate how the same crazy wisdom offers something for today. These women really lived. They really suffered. They have so much to teach.

My purpose? To remind each of us of the ruts we allow ourselves to get into and to suggest that not only are there alternative approaches to our problems but that these alternatives could be more effective. And that there is delight in exploring crazy wisdom. As our trust in this wilder aspect of our lives grows, so will a deepening sense of fun and fearlessness, not to mention a swell of clearheaded joy.

I bow in gratitude to those women who, almost three thousand years ago, got off the floor; shaved their heads; and broke their own rules, habits, and cultural norms and in so doing raised happiness, joy, and delight to new levels.

May all beings be as lucky.

This book is divided into nine chapters. Following an introduction to the women as a group, each of the remaining chapters introduces a difficult situation such as the loss of a spouse, the betrayal of a lover, or facing the pull of an affair. Stories of how the ancients faced these difficulties show up in every chapter. In addition, quotes from the ancients' "enlightenment poems" or personal stories of awakening are inserted all over the place as reminders that awakening is our path no matter what tragedies happen between now and then. Finally, examples of how the same crazy wisdom could work today—or already does—complete each chapter: heart dharma for our survival toolbox.

Chapter One
THE ANCIENTS

In the sixth century before Christ, in the foothills of the
Himalayas, near the present-day border between India
and Nepal, there was a small but prosperous kingdom
ruled by the warrior people Sakya. The capital city of
the kingdom was Kapilavastu, and the land around was
thickly dotted with smaller towns and villages. To the
south of this kingdom lay the country of Kosala, and
beyond that the kingdom of Magadha, in the area of the
modern Indian state of Behar around Rajgir. To the east
lay the land of Koliya, from which came Queen
Mahamaya, the wife of the Sakyan ruler, King
Suddhodana.

—HAMMALAWA SADDHATISSA, *Before He Was Buddha*

IN THE YEAR 560 B.C., Queen Mahamaya gave birth to a
son who was to grow into one of the great spiritual sages of all
time. We know him as Buddha. His is a life well suited to the
best story books. Siddhartha, the beloved son of a ruler, gives
up everything, including a beautiful young wife and child, to
search for the keys to happiness: "Take my clothes and my
jewelry back to my father and tell him and my mother and my
wife that they must not worry. I am going away to seek an
escape from the misery of aging, sickness, and death. As soon

as I have found it, I will return to the palace and teach it to my father, my mother, my wife, my son and everyone else. Then everyone will be truly happy." [1]

Following his renunciation of the princely life and six years of asceticism that included almost starving himself to death, young Siddhartha found his answer to the question of unhappiness in his own experience of complete enlightenment. His consequent message for achieving happiness, called the four noble truths, teaches that life is difficult for everyone and that it is difficult because we are always grasping and craving something we don't have. Buddha promised a way out of our suffering. Called the eightfold path, his "middle way" is basically a set of principles for living a life of deep integrity. Such a life automatically brings compassion, peacefulness, love, and joy. More specifically, the eightfold path calls for right understanding, or seeing life as it really is; right thought, or doing our best not to succumb to anger, greediness, or denial; kind and tolerant speech; actions that demonstrate our respect for all the things and people in our lives (including those we wish lived far away); a livelihood with the same tendencies; giving everything we do everything we've got; mindfulness; and concentration.

For the rest of his life Buddha wandered the three hundred kilometers between the southern edge of the Himalayas and the Ganges, teaching his truths. His was a landscape thick with woods and jungles, complete with tigers, elephants, and rhinos. Wooded areas were broken up by fields of grains and dotted with villages that had grown up alongside slow and easy rivers. This is a geography that still only knows three seasons: so hot your skin itches, a cold similar to a late New England autumn, and monsoon. If you've never experienced a monsoon, it is hard to imagine what this season is like. Torrents of rain fall for hours each day, for weeks at a time. Floods prevent travel, and dirt roads become mud slides. Accompanying the rain? Armies of rats, snakes, and scorpions if you happen to reside at the base of the Himalayas.

Four kingdoms provided support for the young wanderer and his followers. North of the Ganges River was the kingdom of Kosala. Buddha's family came from the city of Kapilavastu, which was right on the northern border of Kosala in the republic of Sakyas. Kosala is where one of Buddha's best pals, King Pasenadi, lived. Southwest of Kosala was Vamsa, home to King Udena and a set of wives who tried to kill each other on a pretty regular basis. To the south of the river was the kingdom of Avanti and to the east of Avanti, Magadha. Buddha and his followers seemed to spend most of their time here. Another of his best friends and later a major donor, King Bimbisara, lived in Magadha. Because his kingdom was prosperous, thanks to iron ore mining, Bimbisara was able to keep Buddha's followers in food and shelter, even as their numbers grew into the thousands. Marriages linked the kingdoms in one way or another, for better or worse. Mostly, a relatively peaceful coexistence was the order of the day, and people could freely cross the borders between the different kingdoms.

Much is known about the first people attracted to the teachings of Buddha. His time period was one where the homeless spiritual seeker was a familiar sight. In the decades before Buddha was born, a spontaneous movement supporting spiritual growth had surfaced. People were starting to break out of the existing spiritual disciplines, with their rituals and caste orientation. What some call "a psychosis of spiritual seeking" had seized the young men of the warrior and merchant classes across the four kingdoms. Thousands abandoned their work and turned their wives and children over to their extended families for safekeeping so they themselves could take on the lifestyle of a wandering ascetic. While the young men's choices of spiritual practices ranged from self-mutilation to vows of complete silence, almost all of them were on a constant look-out for a teacher who could instruct them on genuine spiritual practice.

Along came Buddha. At thirty-six he was an attractive teacher: handsome, smart, obviously from the princely caste—and enlightened. Men, mostly from the ruling class, began to follow him. First they showed up in small groups, then in hundreds, then by the thousands. Young, eager, and bright, they left families and livelihoods to follow Buddha and embrace his teachings, walking from village to village not so much to preach as to demonstrate, by example, the power of Buddha's understanding. Yasa was one of these. The epitome of the idly rich young man, he bumped into Buddha in one of the deer parks where the Buddha would go to meditate. Asking Buddha about himself, Yasa was so struck by the innate joy and wisdom emanating from the monk that he immediately renounced his princely life to search for what Buddha had found—bringing his fifty-four best friends along with him.

Then there were the three Kassapa brothers, "matted-hair ascetics" who had a local monopoly on the spiritual market, with more than a thousand followers between them. Hearing Buddha, they also became disciples. In later years one of the brothers, suddenly realizing how all of what Buddha was teaching could be manifested in a single flower, became Buddha's first dharma heir, responsible for guaranteeing that the teachings survived Buddha's own passing. The sons of the headmen of two villages, Sariputta and Moggallana, also became followers, responsible for translating many of Buddha's words into "the language of the valley," or local idiom, and teaching the growing crowds of followers when Buddha was unavailable.

In the meantime, what about the women? What of their lives? It was bad enough that they had to survive at least two miserable seasons every year. It was bad enough to live in a social system, a caste system, where they were utterly dependent upon their extended families and, for married women, the kindness of their husbands' families. To make matters worse, in addition to facing the natural disasters of their lives—disease, dire poverty, the deaths of beloved relatives—many of the women lost their men—their sons, lovers, husbands, brothers, and fathers—to asceticism. Where did these women fit in?

For Buddha's first few years of teaching, the answer was: nowhere.

But then Ananda surfaced, and he was a surprise advocate for female spiritual seekers. Ananda, Buddha's cousin and attendant in his later years, was a naturally kind and compassionate monk. He cared about everybody's welfare—not just the monks but also women and children. As the women relatives of the first followers of Buddha heard about the men's spiritual experiences studying with the Buddha, many of them wanted to sign up as well.

Ananda watched all of this unfold.

One of those women was Pajapati, Buddha's beloved stepmother. By all accounts Pajapati was a sweet and nurturing parent, nursing the young prince through his childhood and seeing him through his own marriage at sixteen to her cousin, Yasodara. Following Buddha's enlightenment, and after hearing him teach, many of his relatives wanted to become disciples. His father and his six siblings and cousins, all male, were the first group to insist that they be allowed to study with him. Pajapati wanted in as well, but was held back by familial obligations. Then, when Buddha's father, Suddhodana, died in 524 B.C., she finally had the freedom to become a mendicant follower. Determined to become one, and knowing that Buddha had refused all female disciples to date, Pajapati cautiously asked Buddha for permission to become his student. Now elderly, she sought him out in the Nigrodha Grove, just outside Buddha's hometown. "It would be good, she said, if women too could go forth into homelessness in the Dharma proclaimed by you." [2]

Buddha flat-out refused. "Do not be eager to obtain the going forth of women from home to homelessness in the Dhamma and Discipline proclaimed by the Tathagata." [3] His stepmother was crushed. Pajapati talked with female friends and relatives about her yearning only to discover a groundswell of shared feelings. Many women wanted to be nuns, wanted to follow Buddha. Not easily dissuaded, the women began to organize.

The women decided to approach Buddha as a group and formally ask his permission to follow him as traveling mendicants. Three times he rejected their appeal. After the third refusal he and the monks left for Vesali, about a hundred miles away. To demonstrate their spunk and determination, Pajapati and a handful of women followed him anyway. They wanted to prove that they could survive as wanderers as well as the monks could. They cut off their hair and put on the yellow robes of a disciple to show the sincerity of their hope to become disciples.

The group made it to Vesali. When Buddha spotted them, feet swollen, filthy, and crying from exhaustion, he was not happy. Ananda, on the other hand, couldn't bear to see Pajapati treated the way Buddha was treating her. He decided to intercede on behalf of the women. Buddha also said no to him. Three times. "Do not be eager, Ananda, to obtain the going forth of women from home into homelessness in the Dhamma and Discipline proclaimed by the Tathagata." [4]

Ananda refused to take no for an answer. Trying a different tack, he asked Buddha the core question of the time for all women: "Is a woman able to gain the fruit of stream-entry [the experience of no-self] or of once returning [having one more life to go through before enlightenment], or of non-returning [living the last life before enlightenment], or of arahantship [living without desire and hatred and worthy of being worshipped], if she leaves the household life and enters into homelessness in the Dhamma and Discipline of the Tathagata?" [5]

"Yes."

"If a woman is able to do this, Lord—and moreover Mahaprajapati Gotami has rendered great service to the Blessed One: she is his aunt, his governess, and nurse, nourished him with her own milk after his mother died—therefore it would be good if the Blessed One would allow women to leave home for the homeless life in the Dhamma . . ." [6]

Our hero. He got Buddha to admit that women are capable of enlightenment—out loud. Plus, these were the women who had nurtured and cared for the monks so that the men could do their spiritual work. Surely they deserved the same exposure to the teachings.

With trepidation Buddha allowed the women to become followers, opening a whole new vista to them: Constant spiritual practice. Teachings unlike any they had heard before. Different interpretations of their lives. Different priorities to their days. Whole new outlooks on relationships. Different takes on love.

As soon as Pajapati was ordained as a nun she saluted Buddha and stood to one side while he began to teach. Standing there, Pajapati experienced a deep awakening. So profound was her experience that she later let loose with a long prose poem describing the profound change in her life that had already come from studying with Buddha:

> Buddha the waken, the hero, hail!
> Supreme o'er every being that hath life,
> Who from all ill and sorrow hast released
> Me and so many, many stricken folk.
> Now I have understood how I doth come.
> Craving, the cause, in me is dried up.
> Have I not trod, have I not touched the end
> Of ill—The Eightfold Path?
>
> Oh! But tis long I've wandered down
> all time.
> Living as mother, father, brother, son,
> And as grandparent in the ages past—
> Not knowing how and what things really are.
> And never finding what I needed.
> But now mine eyes have seen the Exalted One;
> And now I know this living frame's the last,
> And shattered is th' unending round of births.
> No more Pajapati shall come to be! [7]

It was a new ball game for women.

Thousands followed Buddha during his lifetime. They came from all walks of life and from all classes. Some were royalty, others servants. Many were the mothers or sisters of the monks; a few were abandoned wives. Prostitutes studied beside harem women who studied beside grandmothers. Together, they demonstrated a determination to let go of the junk of their lives, to get past soured relationships, to burrow through the mountains of resentment and negative emotions accumulated over lifetimes. In their wake came fresh views on love and relationships, crazy wisdom for a new millennium, and not a moment too soon.

THE WOMEN

While the women who stumbled into enlightenment weren't as closely related to Buddha as Pajapati, each of the women introduced here, all members of the initial group of followers, has left behind wisdom on how to live happily in a world of relationship samsara (the painful cycle of birth, death, and rebirth).

Known her entire life as one of the most breathtaking beauties in five kingdoms, Ambapali was so astonishingly beautiful that princes fought over her. Their battles finally ended when she was officially appointed chief courtesan of the city of Vesali. In those days, the role of courtesan was considered to be a positive thing. It gave women an inordinate amount of independence relative to wives or other single women. In Ambapali's case, she evolved into a very wealthy business-woman. She also bore a son to Buddha's buddy King Bimbisara and was responsible for building a hermitage where Buddha and his monks spent many of their retreats. Over time, Ambapali watched her livelihood and all of her social support erode as age inevitably robbed her of her identity, not to mention the relationships that had physically and financially supported her for years. She teaches us about impermanence, appreciation, and the fine art of being content.

Capa was the daughter of a trapper who was known for his generous provision of food for many young monks. Capa fell in love with one of them; they married and had a child, but the monk abandoned her to go back to the life of an ascetic. Capa defined love in a whole new way. Out of her deep love for her husband she was able to help him leave her!

Born to a well-to-do family, Citta followed Buddha's teachings for something like fifty years before she finally had her first experience of enlightenment as an old, old woman. Citta teaches us about caring for ourselves first and foremost. Doing no harm starts with the body-mind that has our name on it.

Isadasi was a woman who desperately tried to be the perfect wife, following all the complicated cultural rules of the day—acting toward her husband as a mother, a servant. Despite all her efforts, her husband couldn't stand her and left. She gives us more lessons on working through, and with, abandonment.

Khema was one of the two women responsible for running the first community of nuns. She came from a ruling family and was so beautiful that her skin was described as the color of pure gold. As a young woman she was the chief consort of King Bimbisara, eventually giving up even that relationship for a shot at enlightenment. Khema reminds us that life is much too short. We need to stay clear on what really matters.

Unlike most of the other women, Kisagotami came from a poor family. As a young bride, she was terribly mistreated by her in-laws. When she bore a son she was better treated. She became a model wife and mother until her baby died as a toddler. Insane with grief, Kisagotami went to Buddha, begging him to bring her baby back to life. Her story is about the compassion we all experience that springs from a deep loss. In these places we realize that the most important thing in life is not a relationship with someone else, it is the relationship we have with ourselves. It is how we nurture that relationship.

On the other end of the social scale was Mallika, the queen of Kosala. The spunky and independent-minded wife of King Pasenadi, Mallika cajoled him with so much vehemence to listen to Buddha that he finally gave in to save their relationship . . . and became one of Buddha's disciples himself. Theirs is a long, happy love story. When Mallika dies before her husband, he goes insane with grief. Mallika's story alone could fill a book. She faced jealousy and competition at every turn—the down and dirty, mean and ugly components of relationships, yet she was able to overcome them all.

Patacara was one of the most powerful leaders among the women disciples. A skilled and gifted teacher in her later years, Patacara was one of the few nuns who actually preached to laypeople. Her story is important because it clarifies the appropriateness of women as teachers. Patacara came from a banker's family and was supposed to marry a young man of equal rank; instead, she ran away with her lover, one of the family servants. Basically, her life went downhill from there until she resolved to follow the Buddha, quickly making a name for herself as a disciplined and knowledgeable nun. She teaches about the cost of lust and the need to be clear about what we really mean when we say, or think, we love someone.

Samavati was a prominent laywoman from a merchant family of Bhaddavati. She learned about Buddha from her slave woman Khujjuttara, who spent every cent she had on flowers for a little altar after she heard Buddha's first teaching. Samavati couldn't believe how happy her slave was and had to see what was going on for herself, knowing that following her slave's footsteps could mean giving up her relationships and her social standing. Samavati's story reminds us of an important question: How much do we really need when it comes to relationships? Do we really need to be swept off our feet? Are we really looking for a prince? Was Cinderella a total setup?

Sirima and Uttara were both members of Buddha's harem when he was a young prince. In fact, their lives were more like those of indentured servants. As the story goes, they both loved Buddha so much that they decided to follow him even when they thought he might be completely nuts. While their lives had been difficult in the palace, at least there they had shelter, food, and clothing. The two made a pact to give even these things up to follow Buddha on the chance that he really had something to teach. Happily, he did. Sirima and Uttara teach us the value of friendship between women and the rewards that come with putting our spiritual work at the top of our to-do list.

Again and again we are faced with the same burning question: What really matters?

Subha was a later addition to the group. Born into an eminent Brahmin family in Buddha's hometown, Subha decided at an early age that she wanted to become a nun under Pajapati. When she is almost raped by a man in love with her "beautiful eyes," she blinds herself so he will no longer be attracted to her. Okay, maybe that's a little extreme, but you get her point. Subha teaches us about the distractions that come with beauty and about how we need to be clear about what is truly important in our all too short lives.

Vasuladatta and Magandiya were also consorts of King Udena. Both were actually offered to Buddha as wives when he was young. When he said no, they became wives of King Udena. Apparently they never quite got over Buddha's rejection, at least Magandiya never did. She became so hateful, and so jealous of the king's other wives, that she actually burned her biggest rival to death. That the young woman could commit such a heinous deed and later become a nun is a tribute to the power of salvation in a heart so sincere that it not only wants forgiveness but awakening, too. Her story is a literal reminder that jealousy can kill.

Vimala was the daughter of a prostitute and decided to follow her mother's career path. She was also apparently quite a beauty. So overwhelmed with lust at the first sight of him, Vimala did her darnedest to seduce Moggallana, one of Buddha's top disciples. His response was to call her some pretty horrible names. This so shocked her that she wanted to find out what had given him the ability to reject her. That curiosity led to her becoming a nun and, later, enlightened. Her story reminds us that so much opens up to us when we let go of our need for physical beauty—ours and our partner's.

And finally, there is Visaka. She was the loving wife of an eminent man who, after hearing the Buddha teach, decided he would never touch a woman again. Visaka decided to follow Buddha as well and gave up her social standing for a life of meditation in the country. After some time she returned home to find that her husband had decided not to renounce the world after all. Rather than respond in anger, Visaka became her husband's teacher. Buddha was known to say that she was such a skilled educator that her words were his words. Some people believe that portions of the *Dhammapada*, one of the most well-known collections of Buddha's teachings, are actually the teachings of Visaka. Her story demonstrates the truth of our potential as teachers.

For most of the women who followed Buddha, problems in their relationships caused the pain that led them to him. In most cases, relationships were ripped out from under them for one reason or another. In others, the women themselves walked away from their husband or lover—an awesome act of courage given the time and the place. In each of the 166 stories that have lasted through the centuries, miracle of miracles, enlightenment arrived through each woman's understanding of the impermanence of all of the components of relationships—youth, beauty, well-defined roles, commitment, acceptance. Sometimes enlightenment happened quickly. Other times it took years. Out of these women's lives emerged a deep humility and compassion and a driving need to surrender to the reality of their situations. As a result, "the great ball of doubt" or momentum toward the experience of enlightenment was allowed to grow until at last a deep, secure, and abiding happiness laid at their feet. And we rejoice. Because if they can, you and I can. In the wake of their experiences arose relationship dharma. Wisdom that we can use to figure out our own lives, to set our relationships upright, to find our own awakened hearts.

SOME OF THE WOMEN described in this book have become known to us because their lives show up in Buddha's own teachings. Their sincere efforts, demonstrating an abiding faith in the four noble truths, were so strong that he singled out their behavior as an example to other spiritual seekers. For most of the women, however, the journey of their stories to our place in time was much different, much quieter. These women shared the stories of their enlightenment in the form of prose poems that were memorized and passed along, generation by generation, for some say 350 years. At that point they were finally written onto palm leaves during a major Buddhist council that was held in Sri Lanka somewhere around 80 B.C. Long neglected, the poems resurfaced in 1909 in a translation by a wild woman adventurer named Caroline Rhys David. After that, silence again until K. R. Norman published an academic translation of the Therigatha in 1971. It took another twenty years for Boston-based Susan Murcott to trip over Norman's translation during a stay in Melbourne, Australia, and find the time, heart, and energy to further free the stories from the old texts.

Thank Buddha she did. You and I need the stories of these ancient women. We need them as proof that we *all* have sadness in our lives. We *all* have crises. We *all* have relationship issues. Not a single one of us is safe. Yet in the same breath they offer their lives as proof that we can survive the despair and the heartbreaks. Most of all, these women stand as models for how we can transform our personal tragedies into our own awakening. I cannot imagine a greater gift.

Chapter Two
RELATIONSHIPS AS PARTNERSHIPS

> And why has modern love developed in such a way as to maximize submission and minimize freedom, with so little argument about it? . . . We are more than happy to police ourselves and those we love and call it living happily ever after. Perhaps a secular society needed another metaphysical entity to subjugate itself to after the death of God and love was available for the job. But isn't it a little depressing to think we are somehow incapable of inventing forms of emotional life based on anything other than submission?
>
> — LAURA KIPNIS, *New York Times Magazine*

LAURA KIPNIS IS A PROFESSOR at Northwestern University. She thinks a lot about love. She is very smart and she is very funny and she can wax poetic with the best of them about how screwed up our thinking is when we expect to find lifelong happiness in a relationship with one partner, how deluded we are to continue to believe that we can be sexually attracted to the same person for fifty years. May Buddha bless those few and far between couples capable of doing the psychic and psychological work needed to pull off such a feat. I know I couldn't do it. Even ten years is tough for this Dharma puppy. The rules are just too suffocating: "You can't leave the house without saying where you're going. You can't not say what time you'll return. You can't go out when the other person feels like staying at home. You can't be a slob. . . . You can't gain weight . . . and so on. The specifics don't matter. What matters is that the operative word is 'can't.' Thus is love obtained." [1]

It need not be so. Real partnerships are possible—relationships where "can" and "how can I help?" are the operative phrases.

LOVING PARTNERSHIPS

Ambapali was blessed with beauty, grace, and charm. Men loved her. They fought over her, vied for her hand, until she was finally appointed the city's chief courtesan. Only then did she find peace—mostly, anyway. Apparently, Ambapali became a courtesan in the original sense of the word, as a woman offering and accepting culture and pleasure to more than one person. She was so popular that it is said that the city of Vesali became prosperous solely because of her work and relationships. In turn, Ambapali was generous with her charitable donations, becoming known as the uncrowned queen of the kingdom. She was known for her independence, her sureness about herself, and her view of sexual relationships as partnerships.

One of Ambapali's most frequent patrons was King Bimbisara of Magadha, one of Buddha's earliest followers. As the story goes, Buddha and his retinue were resting in a forest southwest of Rajagaha when Bimbisara, then thirty-one years old, appeared, complete with his own retinue of Brahmins, householders, courtiers, orderlies, and guards. [2] Overhearing a teaching about how peace comes from living a life free from the cravings of sensual pleasures, Bimbisara realized that Buddha was no ordinary teacher and invited him and his followers to a meal the next day.

At that meal the king served the monk and his disciples with his own hands—something that was never done. Following the meal he gave Buddha a huge bamboo wood grove near the northern gate of the city of Rajagaha so Buddha and his entourage would always have a quiet refuge to return to in the rainy season.

The king also asked to become Buddha's disciple. When he was accepted he brought with him followers by the thousands, including Ambapali, who had heard about Buddha from her lover. She was completely struck by the teaching about desire and how grasping and craving for pleasure only leads to trouble. She had seen the consequences of such cravings among the princes who loved her, who were willing to kill each other over her even when she clearly had no interest in a monogamous relationship. Even when she was pregnant with Bimbisara's son, Ambapali held that her independence was too important to settle down with one partner. No asking for permission, no wrestling over how clean a room needed to be, no staying awake because Bimbisara was snoring and she was obligated to stay in his bed. In this way the courtesan kept her charm and beauty fresh for years.

Ambapali was clearly her own woman. And she was deeply respected for her independence. There is a wonderful story about how the Buddha, many years after they had first met, was traveling through Vesali, where Ambapali lived, and stopped at her mango grove to rest. When she heard that he was there, Ambapali quickly went to visit him, to see if she could offer him and his followers food or if there were any other ways she could help them to be more comfortable. In response, Buddha offered her a one-on-one teaching on the four noble truths and eightfold path. Inspired, Ambapali invited him and all his monks to her living quarters for a feast the next day.

As she was leaving, rushing a little because she had so much work ahead of her, a couple of princes from the area stopped her to ask if she was okay. This wasn't the calm courtesan they knew. When Ambapali told them about her encounter with Buddha they begged her to let them host him instead.

Nope.

Figuring that if they go to Buddha themselves he would override Ambapali, the princes tracked him down and invited him to a meal the next day—at their palaces. While it was true that Ambapali was an independent woman, she was still just a woman. They were certain Buddha would accept their offer.

Nope.

Buddha had already accepted Ambapali's invitation. Frustrated, they exclaimed, "We have been defeated by that mango girl! We have been tricked by that mango girl!" [3] Ambapali didn't budge.

Even in the face of the potential wrath and rejection by several of her lovers, the courtesan hosted a wonderfully successful meal. At the end of it she gave the monks her mango grove so that they would have more choices for refuges during the rainy season.

Ambapali followed Buddha for years. When her son by Bimbisara, Vimala Kondanna, grew up, he also became a monk and achieved enlightenment. One day, hearing a sermon from her son, Ambapali decided it was time to do her spiritual work full-time, quickly falling into her own awakeness.

The courtesan's verses of enlightenment reflect a deep understanding of how silly it is to depend on fleeting things for happiness, and her take on physical beauty is particularly powerful:

My hair was black, the color of bees,
Each hair ending in a curl.
Now on account of old age
It has become like fibers of hemp:
Not otherwise is the word
Of the Speaker of Truth.

Covered with flowers my head was fragrant
Like a casket of delicate scent.
Now on account of old age
It smells like the fur of a dog.
Not otherwise is the word
Of the Speaker of Truth . . .

Brilliant and beautiful like jewels,
My eyes were dark blue and long in shape.
Now, hit hard by old age,
Their beauty has utterly vanished.
Not otherwise is the word
Of the Speaker of Truth . . .

Attended by millions of creatures
I went forth in the Conqueror's Teaching.
I have attained the unshakable state,
I am a true daughter of the Buddha.

I am a master of spiritual powers
And of the purified ear-element.
I am, O great sage, a master of knowledge
Encompassing the minds of others.

I know my previous abodes,
The divine eye is purified,
All my cankers have been destroyed,
Now there is no more re-becoming. [4]

It is said that Ambapali was so enlightened that she was able to recollect all of her previous lives, including seeing all the times when she had been a prostitute or a nun. Even in years that were rough, when she had given in to desire and submission, she also saw how she had been capable of tremendous generosity and kindness until, in this lifetime, she had become a true daughter to Buddha's teachings.

Personal Wholeness

When we accept that we are responsible for our own lives, miracles can happen. One of them is that we start shedding all the "shoulds" and start to see our "suchness," or who we really are beneath all the masks and roles. We start to feed the suchness, and the more we feed it the happier we become.

Every year I sit down to write a vision of what I expect my life to be in five years—an authentic life without "shoulds," without masks. On a blank piece of paper I write the following categories down the left side of the page:

- home
- work
- relationships
- art
- spiritual effort
- what else?

Then I give myself ten minutes to write about each topic. For the category "home," the writing begins with the phrase: "In five years, I'll live . . ." And then I let her rip. Whatever comes out, comes out. My hand gallops across the page as fast as I can move it. I don't stop for anybody or anything. This includes grammar, punctuation, and spelling.

When the timer goes off I start the second section: "In five years I'll be . . ." That section is about livelihood. Where will the money come from to pay the bills? Next section: "In five years the relationships in my life will include . . ." For art, I write about music, drawing, and writing. Then, "In five years, spiritually . . ." Finally, to make sure that nothing has been left out of the vision, I always end with ten minutes for answering the question "Anything else?" Looks like I'll have a puppy somewhere in the next three years. His name will be Spot.

This is a deeply comforting exercise. It offers an instant taste of wholeness and always stirs up excitement in its doing. Best of all, anytime I need to make a decision related to any of these topics, I can always ask myself which choice will move my life in the direction of the vision. In that way the visions become reality.

There's more. The exercise itself provides visible proof that not only are we responsible for our own lives, but the very act of taking responsibility opens our hearts so excitement can seep in. This is the same excitement that we feel when our spiritual practice deepens. The two feed each other.

It was Ambapali's personal wholeness that was so attractive to the princes and to King Bimbisara—her absence of neediness and her ability to leave any relationship that did not respect her independence as a woman. Ambapali lived her relationships as partnerships, not as subjugation. She was independent, clear about what mattered to her, and fearless when it came to disagreeing with her lovers. When she wanted to care for Buddha and his followers, she didn't ask anyone's permission. When she decided to follow him herself, again she asked no one's permission. When she decided to give him a mango grove, it was her own choice. This independence never cost her suitors or patrons. Ironically, it was the combination of her independence, feistiness, and beauty that kept suitors coming to her door until, as an elderly woman, she decided to take a vow of chastity as a nun.

Ambapali realized that she was responsible for her own life. Period. We forget that sometimes. No matter what, in the end, you and I are responsible for ourselves. No one else. Not our husbands, lovers, partners. When we admit to this responsibility and embrace it, all sorts of barriers to spiritual growth and healthy relationships fall away.

Wholeness
Personal wholeness feeds healthy relationships, because it enables us to let go of our craving to have our partners meet so many of our needs. Back when I was way too young to be married, when I was twenty-three (I now happen to believe that the best age for a first marriage is about thirty), I not only married a hunk of a lover but I also immediately (a) got pregnant, and (b) moved two thousand miles away from my family.

Within weeks I was depending on my husband for everything. I couldn't wait for him to get home from school to ask him about his day. And his answer could never just be "good"—I wanted the minutia. How many students had shown up for each class? What did the professor say exactly? What did he think about what the professor said? Did he have any homework? What was it? Would he like some company while he did it?

To his credit, mostly because his mother apparently raised him to be a martyr, he would answer the questions patiently—every night. Then, after dinner, when all he wanted was some quiet time, I was ready to get out of the house. Could we go to a movie, or for a short hike, or even to the grocery store? Since he was the only person I knew, I fully expected him to go with me, and when he occasionally begged off, I was devastated.

We almost didn't make it.

After a year I was so miserable and lonely that I went back to school—to graduate school—just to be around other people. Suddenly, a marriage that had deteriorated so badly that my husband had fallen into an affair with a fellow student (the bitch), began to pick up again. The affair ended, I spent most of my free time with friends, and we fell in love at a slightly more mature level. What still fascinates me is that he didn't end the affair until I was psychologically independent—until I had found my own path and rediscovered a sense of wholeness without his help.

All kinds of partnerships are possible when we are whole. One of the best marriages I have ever known was a husband and wife who literally lived next door to each other. The Portland, Oregon, couple had built two almost identical houses side by side on a lot. They lived independently until one or the other was invited in—for a meal, conversation, a slumber party. She had a job in social work. He was an artist. They had their own friends and a couple of shared ones. Sometimes they took vacations together and sometimes they didn't. When I met them I remember being struck by how kind and considerate they were of each other. Nothing was taken for granted.

Psychological independence keeps us interesting. It protects us from potential abuse because, as independent women, staying in a relationship is always a choice. It feeds a confidence that can be sexier than the perfect body.

RELATIONSHIP RULES

Like most of my woman friends, I have spent much of my adult life searching for tools that genuinely help to sustain both love relationships and independence. Tools that promote relationships as partnerships. Over the years, I've discovered that, communication skills aside, the best tools are internal to both partners and promote the intention of honoring and protecting the relationship as it grows and evolves. What you and I really need are anchors independent of the relationship. What anchors? Unchanging ones, anchors that are "true" not only in the context of loving another person but that are helpful in the other dimensions of our lives as well. When I started to look for anchors from the larger perspective of feeding all parts of us, choices suddenly narrowed down to a handful or less.

At first I zeroed in on the Golden Rule—treat others as you would like to be treated—for its simplicity. But then I took it out of the running. I don't know about you, but I don't always want to be treated the way my partner wants to be treated. Here's just one example, so trite it could make *The Man Show*. Someone I'd known intimately for years liked to go to sleep right after sex. Me? I wanted to talk, cuddle, analyze our lives, make future plans. The Golden Rule positioned us for an argument every single time one of us brought it up as a potential relationship ground rule.

I kept looking. Buddhism and the Buddhist precepts, while

they go a long way in feeding world peace, did not give me tools for feeding an intimate relationship, although they did provide a broad refuge. Not lying; not taking what isn't given to us; not engaging in promiscuous sex; not muddying our minds with too much alcohol, drugs, or whatever—all useful. After an embarrassingly long time, given that they are pasted onto the front of my refrigerator, I landed on the six paramitas, or perfections. A core part of Buddha's teachings, the paramitas are sort of like oil you can throw on a fire to help it to burn brighter. They are typically introduced as behaviors that strengthen spiritual practice. They also happen to be terrific catalysts when it comes to building relationships as partnerships.

> May I be generous and helpful.
> May I be pure and virtuous.
> May I be patient. May I be able to bear and forbear the wrongs of others.
> May I be strenuous, energetic, and persevering.
> May I practice meditation and attain concentration and oneness to serve all beings.
> May I gain wisdom and be able to give the benefit of my wisdom to others.

Jackpot.

All the ancients who followed Buddha lived by the paramitas. Starting with Ambapali.

May I Be Generous and Helpful

I've always loved weddings. Partly it's because weddings are so beautiful. Brides always glow. Grooms always weep. Love permeates the air like a drug. Now, one of the perks of being a dharma teacher is that I get to go to between three and six weddings each year—as the minister. It is the single most enjoyable thing I do. The ceremonies are a celebration of life and its possibilities, always filled with excitement and a determination on the part of the couple to make their union one that lasts. Usually the couple asks me for advice—despite my own spotty personal history. My response, and the gift that I give to couples, whatever their spiritual tradition, is a small paperback book by the Vietnamese Zen master Thich Nhat Hanh called *Touching Peace*. While it is not a book focused solely on personal relationships, it has some of the best advice of any I've encountered. And all of it has to do with the six paramitas and how we need to see our partner as precious, whatever our circumstances. Here's a taste:

> We can do this. We see that the other person, like us, has both flowers and compost inside, and we accept this. Our practice is to water the flowerness in her, and not bring her more garbage. We avoid blaming and arguing. When we try to grow flowers, if the flowers do not grow well, we do not blame or argue with them. We blame ourselves for not taking care of them well. Our partner is a flower. If we take care of her well, she will grow beautifully. If we take care of her poorly, she will wither. To help a flower grow well, we must understand her nature. How much water does she need? How much sunshine? We look deeply into ourselves to see our true nature, and we look into the other person to see her nature. . . . We can sit down, hold our partner's hand, look deeply at him, and say, "Darling, do I understand you enough? Do I water your seeds of suffering?

Do I water your seeds of joy? Please tell me how I can love you better." [5]

Loving someone better is about mindfulness, about doing the small things that matter, not the big things. Just because. Maybe it's showing up with her favorite cup of coffee when you spontaneously stop by where she works. Maybe it's running an errand for him because he doesn't have time to get to the ATM machine, the accountant's, and then home at a decent hour for dinner together. Feeding each other's essence is as much about surprise acts of kindness as it is about abiding to the negotiated parameters of the relationship. It is your turn to make dinner and your partner just happens to show up with a ready-made meal of your favorite foods. It works, right?

The Buddha taught, over and over and over, that generosity is the first door we walk through if we are serious about our spiritual work. Without generosity enlightenment is flat-out impossible. We're too self-centered. Unless our relationships are bathed in generosity they don't have a chance. At the other extreme, generosity can buttress a faltering relationship, giving the other paramitas time to work their magic. It fuels the little extras, the surprise moments that keep us fresh and interesting. And it demonstrates our regard for each other, whatever we're going through together.

When I was working on my doctoral dissertation, one of the tasks I committed to doing was walking door-to-door in an inner-city neighborhood to do random interviews with the families that lived there. It was pretty scary to a twenty-six-year-old. I had spent many of my formative years in Australia, where strangers simply do not knock on your door—ever.

Here I was breaking my own rules of etiquette. Plus, I didn't have any idea who lived behind the doors. Maybe Jack the Ripper was still alive. Who could say?

On the other hand, it was obvious that doing the interviews would provide the "primary data" (i.e., "from the horse's mouth" information) I needed to make my point that a particular federal loan program was helping families to remain in a fast-gentrifying neighborhood. One of the most generous things anyone has ever done for me was my husband getting out of bed with me early each morning before I left. He'd give me the pep talk I needed. On some days, without saying anything, he'd get dressed and get in the car and drive me into the neighborhood, waiting outside through each interview even though he had his own full day of work ahead of him. While we never talked about it, his wide-open generosity told me more about how much he loved me than any bouquet of flowers ever did.

He was so generous and helpful, that man. It was magic for our marriage and got us through more relationship samsara than I care to remember.

May I Be Pure and Virtuous

Trust matters. In partnerships between independent people, trust matters because we are each living self-contained lives in the middle of a shared future. If I can't trust you in an intimate relationship, particularly one that incorporates spirituality into its ether, then the relationship is doomed. Period. And until courtesans come back into vogue, monogamy matters.

I don't care what anyone else says. In my experience, adultery or any other behavior that betrays the concepts of "pure and virtuous" destroys relationships, even those in which the partners agree that monogamy is unnecessary. Buddha was a broken record on this:

> Indulging in transient pleasures
> While failing to do the real work
> of our lives
> leads us to envy the ones
> who have
> spent time and energy on their
> spiritual work . . . [6]

There is something about betrayal that destroys a relationship in its heart. I've seen, been with, and lived through forgiving people who've crossed that boundary. To this day I remain convinced that things are never quite the same afterward, even when the couple agrees to move through a healing process for the sake of the marriage or relationship. If I am in a relationship that is a partnership, my partner and I need to openly, publicly, and loudly commit to virtue and act accordingly. If we can't, then we have to stop pretending we're in a committed, intimate relationship, because we aren't.

Virtue is tough. Loyalty can suck. Attractive people are everywhere. Sex and sensual pleasures are in the air. When we feel ourselves drawn away from our partner it is critical to ask ourselves, just as the ancient women did: What really matters? If we discover we can't stay steady, then commit to getting out of the partnership or reframing it as friendship. At least stop pretending that we are being "pure and virtuous" when we aren't. I hate to think of the karmic consequences of that particular dance.

May I Be Patient. May I Bear and Forbear the Wrongs of Others

One of the great surprises of partnerships like Ambapali's is that we can be more patient with our partners. Back in the days when I only knew complete dependency as a marriage model, every wrong move on the part of my husband made me impatient. He wasn't perfect. I was concerned. Concern morphed into irritation pretty quickly. On days when all I had to look forward to was watching the four toddlers I baby-sat, even small irritations grew into marriage-threatening themes. That's what dependency does.

With independence we can shrug off irritations, because they are only one part of this parade we call life. We don't have hours to dwell on nuances of meaning, because our days are filled with other people, places, and things. I watch my friend Deborah with her partner, Drew. They have been in love for about three years now. Their public displays of affection continue unabated. Deborah is, by nature, not a patient woman. She makes decisions quickly and doesn't take any flak from the contractors who share her world. She isn't a woman you would expect to be patient with a partner. And yet she is. Dinners he's late for, forgotten phone calls, miscues about rendezvous are shrugged off without much more than a grimace. She has plenty to keep her busy, and every surprise loss in their plans to be together becomes an opportunity for her to fill that time slot with a different activity she enjoys—reading, gardening, cooking.

For their first year together I wondered about her flexibility and willingness to keep pretty much all irritations on an "it's no big deal" plane. Over time I've noticed that her patience and willingness to bear and forbear both of their mistakes has somehow transformed Drew's behavior. He is late less often and calls when he says he will. Surprise bouquets of flowers and garden tools appear. After three years he remains head over heels in love with this independent woman, cowgirl boots, pickup, and all.

Patience. One of my best friends in the whole world, Alice, has been married to the same man for almost thirty years, I think. She had heard about him before they met—he was the wild man of their overlapping friendship circle. Finally, at a toga party, they were introduced. That he wasn't wearing anything under the toga was an added bonus, she says. At the time, Alice was a Victorian beauty with porcelain skin, fathomless eyes, and waist-long hair. In the years they have been together they have been through just about everything two people can go through. What has struck me the entire time has been their patience with each other, and with the relationship. Even at her most frustrated, Alice only has kind things to say about her husband. To this day, he would lie down and die for her. I'm sure of it.

When I ask Alice how they've made it this far, her answer is always "patience," even when she doesn't actually say the word. She talks about waiting out the tough times because, in the end, they are both good people who love each other. Hearing her, I think of all the times I've shrugged off relationships because of impatience. Times got a little rough—or worse, boring. (This is all pre-Zen, of course!) Patience would have helped me through my Cinderella reactions to imperfect partners. It would have helped me to stay put long enough to see what someone was really like behind the crisis of the moment.

At the same time, patience protects us when we let go of relationships that just plain don't work. When my Aussie husband made it clear that he couldn't live in the United States—for valid reasons—and I had the courage to say I couldn't immigrate with my then preteen daughter, we both knew our marriage wasn't going to make it. Because he is patient and because I love him, we were able to unweave the marriage, annul it actually, in a way that protected our friendship. To this day, if I ever make it to Queensland, his is the phone number I'll call for suggestions for places to stay, eat, and surf.

May I Be Energetic and Persevering

When I was at Deloitte and Touche, an international management consulting and accounting firm, there was a manager, Allison, who always struck me as being a natural-born leader. A young, athletic-bodied woman, she made decisions quickly and easily, didn't take criticisms personally, and took on the toughest assignments with something that looked suspiciously like eagerness. Much of the time, her assignments kept her away from her husband day and night, for weeks at a time.

One day I asked her how her husband dealt with her absences. I knew the track record for marriages of female management consultants wasn't good. Earlier that morning I had sat in on a managers' meeting and noted that, while all the men were married, all the women, except Allison, were single. Most of us had been married but weren't anymore. One of the younger women—bright and beautiful just so you know—had never been in a long-term relationship. And there was Allison. So I was curious.

She told me her husband was completely supportive of her work. They had a real partnership, she said. When I asked how this was possible, she responded that it had to do with how they met. Three years earlier, overweight, she had decided to ride a bike across the country, east to west, as her way of slimming down. Along the way she met her husband. Although he didn't need to lose weight, he was also riding a bike cross-country. For the first few states she didn't like him at all, but it was safer to be with another person. Plus, her energy and effort were going into the biking.

By the second batch of states they were friends, working hard together, still concentrating on the bikes. By Colorado she was in love. When they hit California he asked her to marry him. What brought them together was their shared energetic effort. It was a surprise aphrodisiac. Physically putting all of themselves into the trip was just plain sexy.

I see it all the time at retreats. People who might never notice one another on the street or in a different environment are working side by side. Maybe it's scrubbing floors or sanding them. Maybe it's composting or building stupas together. Whatever the task, the energy put into it has a way of transforming interactions. People fall in love. Allison stayed in love because she continued to put the bike ride energy into her marriage. So when she and her husband were together, they focused on each other and usually did something athletic together, like hike, climb, or ride. And they remembered how much they cared about each other: enough to give each other the space of work independence.

There is something quite wonderful about putting lots of energy into the known aspects of our lives: "I spent the entire work period every day at an exercise session. . . . I did back bends and stretches while changing the linen; I twisted my body rhythmically to sweep floors; I hung sequentially from each vertebra in my back to scour the toilet; I squeezed the

Windex bottle with all five fingers, alternating my hands to wash the windows. I breathed fully and deeply to set a rhythm for my body movements. After a few weeks of this activity I was exhilarated and bursting with energy." [7]

Virya, energy, is just plain appealing. In this place a person's movements are beautiful, like a spontaneous dance. And there is an authenticity, an openness, almost a vulnerability, about these moments that feeds relationships, because one partner isn't being needy or judging. Instead, she is simply doing what she is doing and no more. But also no less.

Buddha's women followers gave relationships everything they had. They heard him literally and were clearly good students. Their energy never lessened, not when they were hungry or tired, not when they were thirsty or sick. It didn't let up when they were crowded together in small huts during the rainy season or when they made protocol mistakes.

This is the energy that feeds relationships. It tells the person we love that he or she matters to us. One of the few pieces of advice I listened to when I was married, and one that served me well, was that I should treat every day like it was the last one we would have together, to pretend that I would never see my husband again. This advice came from one of my dharma brothers, a man who lives in Mexico City, where there is so much person-to-person crime that, too often, couples really don't see each other again after they kiss good-bye in the morning. It was useful advice. It reminded me to pay attention, told me to take the time to put on clean clothes and wash my hair even when I was only going to see a handful of little kids that day. Virya is the energy that helps us to hear the family stories for the hundredth time with fresh ears and genuine smiles. In my case, virya energy reminded me not to take anything for granted. While other aspects of our marriage eventually deteriorated, energetic effort kept our sexual relationship exciting, spunky, and interesting, without the need for whips and chains.

Virya paramita means slogging through the valleys that happen in any intimate relationship. If you were raised on Cinderella like me, it may not even occur to you that there will be valleys in a relationship. But there always are. Energetic effort provides the booster shot that keeps us going through the reality of love until we can establish higher ground.

May I Practice Meditation and Attain Concentration and Oneness to Serve All Beings

A psychologist once told me that relationships depend far more on who we are than on whom we choose. I'm sure this is true. One of the problems we face in relationships is that we think we know who we are when we don't. Before I started meditating I thought of myself as calm, kind, patient, and informal. Also humorous. If you had asked me what I brought to my relationship I would have listed those attributes. Then an eye twitch, two actually, drove me to meditation. Sitting in a quiet meditation hall, trying my best to quietly breath in and out, I got the surprise of my life. My thoughts weren't kind and I wasn't calm. I fretted, complained, and ranted all the way through my first few years (yup, *years*) of meditating. To this day I have no idea why I thought I was calm. And intense, thy name is *moi*.

One of Buddhism's most famous Zen masters, Dogen, taught that studying Buddhism means studying ourselves first. That's what Buddha's women disciples did. And it is what you and I do when we sit quietly, allowing our minds to show us who we really are, what we're really like. Happily, having a sense of humor was pretty accurate. But I've had to learn to stop worrying so much. If he's late, it doesn't mean he's dead or has run into his ex-wife. And I'm calmer, which means that I actually hear the end of sentences. Patience is slowly showing its face, and kindness . . . okay, kindness has always been there.

The point is that we need to really know *what* we're bringing into a relationship or situation and *whom* we're bringing into it. As long as I was portraying myself as calm and patient, when I was neither, I was setting up my partner. He expected something that didn't exist. It must have been like trying to have a relationship with a full-body mask—an impossible undertaking. When I didn't have a clear picture of myself I shot miscues into the air all day. When I asked a friend, "When will I see you again?" and he answered, "Sometime next week," he assumed that was a perfectly fine answer, given my calm "Okay." What he didn't know was that I had instantly kicked into analysis paralysis trying to figure out all the secret meanings and messages behind his casual response. Happily, meditating caused huge shifts in my behavior—for the better. If I'm unsure about a response I ask for clarification, for concrete responses. "Oh, by Friday I'll hear from you? Perfect." The difference in my interactions with people is enormous.

May I Gain Wisdom and Be Able to Give the Benefit of My Wisdom to Others

Prajna is wisdom, about seeing into the heart of a situation. This is not a wisdom of intelligence but of clarity. When we get rid of some of the murkiness in our brains—the opinions, fears, and melodrama—clarity shows up. And when we bring that clarity or prajna into our relationships, we know intuitively what needs doing. We know what will protect and build a relationship that feeds us and what actions and thinking will create the least harm should we leave a relationship.

Prajna protects compassion. Master Dogen taught that there are really four wisdoms: generosity, or giving without expecting anything in return; loving words; goodwill; and identifying with whatever the other person is going through. When all four are introduced into a relationship, whatever the situation, things get better. This does not necessarily mean that the relationship survives. It may mean going out on our own because we know that we deserve a relationship that offers a partnership of respected equals.

When I was first falling in love with meditation, my boyfriend was very patient with my "stinky Zen." As far as I was concerned, every moment between us was a Zen moment, reflecting the truths of the patriarchs one way or another. The longer I sat, though, the more obvious it became that he and I weren't going to make it. Our world views were just too far apart. At the time, I was headed (although I didn't realize it yet) for a three-year seminary, and he was headed for the Michigan Militia.

He broke up with me.

But he did it with such wisdom that I love him to this day. For the year we were together he was always generous, even to the point of driving me to the temple at four forty-five on some mornings so I could sit with the temple residents. Even as he told me that he knew we weren't going to work, he said it with such tenderness that it actually took a couple of minutes for his words to sink in. His reasons for the breakup were completely motivated by goodwill. He honestly cared about what was best for both of us. He wasn't willing to get in my way and, frankly, wasn't interested in my being worried about his way. He sat with me for what felt like days, waiting for my response, holding me while I cried. The thing is, I knew he was right. Even if it broke my heart.

We still run into each other. Each time it's like seeing an old friend. To this day I am convinced that we are okay with each other because of the deep, compassion-filled wisdom he demonstrated on my couch that night.

HOLDING ON TO THE FRIENDSHIP

One of the heartbreaks of a broken relationship is that we so often lose a good friend when it is clear that the romantic relationship no longer works. It needn't be so. When we leave relationships with our hearts clear, friendships can survive. For most of us (hopefully it isn't just me!) this means giving up anger, greed, and delusion—Buddhism's three poisons. We have to give up the righteous anger that pretty much always follows having been wronged—even if we were the ones to call it quits. (I've never known a woman to be other than righteously angry at the end of a relationship . . . okay, maybe once, but she was a long-term Zen master.) We have to give up wanting something we can no longer have—a sexual relationship, for example. And we have to give up our deluded hope of reconciliation on our own terms. Freed from these three components, we can stay friends.

Beth and Doug Stone have been divorced since 1986. Until his recent death Doug lived in New Hampshire, Beth in greater Los Angeles. "It's always a shock to people that we're so close, that Doug and I were still friends and went places together when he was here. He was my ex-husband of sixteen years . . . we talked on the phone once a day at least, if not twice. When I had a problem, I called him. When I had a good thing to tell him, I called him. One night I was playing Trivial Pursuit with a bunch of friends. It must have been three o'clock his time. I didn't know the answer so I called him. He'd call just to tell me a joke. To chitchat." [8]

Theirs was a partnership—a bond that neither was willing to break—inside or outside of marriage. They visited each other, supported each other, were the best of friends: "There wasn't any reason to remarry. The fact that I had so much support from Doug, emotionally and financially, helped me become independent vicariously. Going through a divorce and raising a boy on your own you become stronger. You find out how much more you can do on your own. . . . He was my confidant. And vice versa. He always had a level head and was always able to make me think clearer." [9] The two had managed to create a relationship that both were willing to protect by letting go of the anger, greed, and delusion that corner us if we let them. Unmarried, their partnership was a match even the gods would envy. When Doug died on September 11, a passenger on one of the flights out of Boston that was flown into the World Trade Center, Beth was devastated. What a world it would be if we all felt the same way about our former partners.

There are many benefits related to staying friends with former lovers. First off, even when you think you're finished with the relationship, you aren't. There is always unfinished business. Just when you think you have all your own stuff you'll remember that your favorite pair of shoes is in his closet. It's easy to ask a friend to drop them off, leave them by the door, or let you run by to get them. And those paychecks you're waiting for? They don't get forwarded by someone who wants revenge or is too saddled with guilt to change the address on the envelope. Where children are involved, remaining friends can make the difference between a little therapy and a lifetime of it for them.

Remaining friends allows us to keep the good memories without feeling guilty. And keeps someone in our safety net who is capable of catching mice in a live trap or listening through the article before we mail it off to the literary journal. When we separated, staying friends with my son's father was enormously helpful. He helped me to find an apartment. Moved furniture for me. And when I fell flat on my face when I returned to dating, he was the person I called. And because he knows me so well, I believed him when he told me I deserved better and that the guy was clearly a psychopath.

So stay friends if you can. How? By remembering that deep down inside we all just want to be happy. And that underneath the mountain of mistakes we all make, people are basically good. This is someone who has loved you. And has done his or her best. Write down all of his positive attributes and tuck them away in a drawer for the next time you start getting really angry. We sometimes think that if we make our former mate a bad guy, our heartbreak will be less. But it won't. The rage just postpones the mourning. A waste of time I say. Better to live with a wide-open broken heart. At least this way, though you may lose a mate, you salvage a friendship. Plus you'll heal a whole lot faster.

A WONDERFUL THING HAPPENS when we stick with our spiritual practice. Our breath becomes our home. Quiet is ours. In that quiet, prajna. When we are having a tough emotional time, we can take refuge in this great quiet, we can tap into never-ending wisdom. So we don't need someone else to give us answers or complete our lives. We can do our own work. From this place you and I can bring the possibility of a true partnership to a relationship. One free of neediness. These are the relationships that last, and these are the ones that provide sustenance to both parties through their last breaths. Maybe longer.

Chapter Three
RELATIONSHIP RAGE

Anger is like a chariot
wildly careening.
A person who can curb her anger
is a true charioteer
while
the rest of us merely hold on to
the reins of the chariot.

Overcome anger with loving kindness.
Overcome evil with good deeds.
Overcome stinginess with generosity.
Overcome lies with truth.

Don't give in to anger.

—*The Still Point Dhammapada*

RELATIONSHIP RAGE IS at an all-time high. Maybe it's just
that there are more of us on the planet. All I know is this:
Rage is completely painful. Screaming, pushing, shoving,
sulking, manipulating, emotional blackmailing, silently smol-
dering, watching for ways to get even. All rage. And uncon-
trollable: You never know where it will aim itself.

A week ago, a young woman, Elizabeth, asked to speak to

me following a Sunday-morning meditation service. She was in tears. She wanted my advice about an incident that had happened to her during the week. She and her partner were driving down a street near her house when they suddenly noticed a couple having an argument. The man started beating the woman, really beating her. Liz wanted to stop to help, but her boyfriend said no—the guy could have a gun or a knife. What should she have done?

My reaction was immediate. Distract the man. Maybe drive a little too close. Or honk the horn and wave wildly. Or just turn the music up to full volume. Shout something nonsensical. Anything that would distract him enough to allow her to get away. And call the police.

Only days before, I had seen an exact replica of her story. I was walking down Cass Avenue, dropping off flyers at the Cass Café and Avalon Bakery in downtown Detroit. Halfway between them I ended up following a couple who were in a heated argument. Suddenly the man hit the woman right across the face. I was shocked still. So was the woman. But then she hit him back. He grabbed her. I ran up behind them. "Hey! Do you know where Avalon is?"

I thought they'd both hit me. The man said "fuck off," which is Cass Corridor slang for "no." But he stopped hitting the woman. She looked at me like I was the most ignorant thing she had yet to see in this lifetime. But she stopped swinging.

Here's the thing. Relationship rage is everywhere. You know it. I know it. When we see it the easiest thing to do is ignore it. But it will only grow if we do. So the real question to ask ourselves is, How can I be helpful in this situation? Sometimes it's best to stay clear of the couple but call the police. Often it's helpful to act as a distraction, even a silly one. I'm guessing that you'll know what to do if you listen to your heart. If your response stops someone from harming, you've just earned a Girl Scout stripe in Tusita heaven.

THE CONSEQUENCES OF RAGE

Buddha's contemporary King Udena was married to some feisty women. One of them, Magandiya, while graceful in figure, beautiful in appearance, and charming when she wanted to be, was also jealous and mean-spirited. When she didn't like another one of his wives, she went after her big time, using relationship rage as her weapon. Her main target was Samavati, the king's favorite consort. Magandiya constantly came up with schemes aimed at stirring the king's wrath toward her competition. Once she told the king that Samavati and her maids had made holes in the walls of the women's living quarters. Although he was irritated, the king didn't punish Samavati. Next Magandiya put a snake into the king's favorite lute and covered the hole with a bunch of flowers. When he picked up the lute to take it with him to Samavati's quarters, she tried to stop him on the pretext that she had a premonition that something harmful was about to happen to him. She warned him that Samavati could be pretty weird. He needed to be careful.

At the door of Samavati's quarters Magandiya, following the king, took the flowers out of the lute. Out came the snake, hissing away. When the king saw the snake he was furious. Deciding that Magandiya was right about Samavati, he finally lost it. The king commanded Samavati to stand in front of him with all of her ladies-in-waiting behind her. Then he put an arrow dipped in poison into his bow.

And shot it.

Since this is an early Buddhist story, and there are miracles in early Buddhist stories, the queen didn't die. And since Samavati and her ladies bore no ill will against the king and stood there filled with loving kindness for him, the arrow missed them, even though the king was an excellent archer.

Would that we were all so lucky. We say to ourselves, "I would never get angry like that," but just watch what happens when someone cuts in front of us in a movie line or on a highway. Listen to the tone of our voices when we get yet another telemarketing phone call during dinner. It's in there. And these aren't even the intimate relationships in our lives, where we've given ourselves permission to openly emote.

Admitting that we have the capacity to rage opens the door to learning how to be more like Samavati. Since I know I can rage with the best of them, and I know the damage done by rage, I can admit that I need to train myself so I won't give in to it when a relationship goes sour. How? By paying close attention to my own emotional patterns. When am I easily triggered? When I'm hungry? Tired? Too busy? It is embarrassingly easy to spot trigger points when we look. I for one need to stop difficult relationship discussions when I'm hungry or tired. Period. They'll only go downhill. It doesn't even matter if they started on an upbeat.

When I was married, my husband refused to have any meaningful conversations with me when the moon was full because, he said, I would invariably ask for a divorce. I didn't believe him until I started paying attention to my thoughts and emotions by keeping a daily journal. He was right. Maintaining quiet times around those days in the lunar calendar gave us years of marital calm.

Journals are powerful tools for releasing rage. The most effective method I know is to simply write "I am so furious . . . " at the top of a page and then let loose. There is only one rule: Don't put your pen down until you are emotionally spent. This can take three pages or thirty. The trick is to just keep writing until you don't have anything else to say. Then go for a walk. It will feel wonderful, and your head will be clear enough to better protect you—and the people around you— from hiding snakes in lutes.

RECOGNIZING RAGE AS HEARTBREAK

Even during Buddha's time, relationship rage was like an explosion that took no prisoners. Kana Mata was a devoted follower of the Buddha. Her married daughter, also named Kana, was visiting when her husband sent a message asking her to please come home. Kana Mata asked her daughter if she would stay a little longer, say a day or two, so the mother and daughter could bake some cakes for the younger Kana to take home with her.

They baked the cakes.

Instead of packaging them up for the younger Kana's husband, they gave them to some monks who stopped by on an alms round. For three days in a row Kana Mata gave her cakes to monks passing by instead of her daughter. At the end of the third day the younger Kana received a second message from her husband. He had taken another wife.

She was beside herself with rage. But instead of being furious with her mother or her husband, Kana took her feelings out on the monks. They had ruined her marriage! Every monk who made the mistake of walking within screaming distance got an earful. She screamed and yelled and screamed some more. Finally, Buddha heard about the young woman and went to see her himself. Had the monks taken anything that wasn't given to them? No. Kana suddenly realized what was going on. She was furious. Heartbroken. Filled with rage.

Sometimes relationship rage is simply our own heart breaking open. This was true for Kana. For some reason it is easier to rage than to weep at our loss. Except that fury cuts such wide swaths of negative karma, because it pulls other people into our melodrama. Innocents: monks, children, pets, neighbors, strangers. At the end of a relationship, when rage starts to erupt—and believe me, you'll feel it coming if you pay close attention to your body—our job is to shout to ourselves, "Stop!" Right then and there we need to ask ourselves what is really going on. In the quiet space right behind the question we'll hear the answer—that our heart has just been split open by a huge emotional loss. And it hurts. It really hurts. This simple realization reminds us that our job is to heal our hearts, not harm other people. In that split second we can give ourselves permission to start the process of healing without wasting precious time doing anything else. We can promise ourselves quiet time. Take ourselves into the woods where nature can give us refuge and we can wail ourselves hoarse. We can buy ourselves flowers and list all the things we admire about ourselves, starting with "I have the courage to love someone with my whole heart." We can list the relationship danger signs we didn't see so we'll be more skillful next time. Or we can decide to simply move on. Movies with sad endings are great triggers for weeping because mostly that is what we need to do at first. We need to weep our eyes dry, without apology, because we're worth it. Before long our lives will be ready to start up again in a fresh and—dare I say it—happy way.

If you need extra motivation to release your rage in a non-harming way, there is this: Even as far back as 537 B.C., the physician Galen connected rage with depression and disease. Rage is different from healthy anger. In situations where we can stay clear about our experience, we will confront what makes us angry and set some boundaries. "When you show up two hours later than you say you will on Friday nights, I feel disrespected, and to protect myself I'll stop planning to see you on Fridays." This is anger. Plotting to hurt the person or something he or she owns? Or someone else? Rage.

THE VALUE OF PERSPECTIVE

Queen Mallika was the spunky and independent-minded wife of King Pasenadi of Kosala. Both were followers of Buddha. Their relationship started on an auspicious note: She was the daughter of Srimala, a laywoman so wise that Buddha later predicted that she would be reborn as the bodhisattva Samantaprabha. Mallika, her daughter, was beautiful and clever, well-behaved, and a source of joy to her parents. As the story goes, just after her sixteenth birthday, Mallika was visiting some flower gardens when she first saw Buddha. So struck was she by his calmness and beauty that she gave him all the food in her picnic basket. He smiled at her and told her that one day she would be the Queen of Kosala.

No way.

She was from the wrong caste. Too low for queen by a long shot.

But Buddha is Buddha for good reasons. When he made predictions they came true. Sure enough, soon afterward King Pasenadi was returning from an exhausting battle with a neighboring king, Ajatasatta (a bad guy if ever there was one;

killed his own father to get the throne). On his way through town, Pasenadi heard someone singing in the city flower garden. It was Mallika.

In a scene right out of Disney, he was so enchanted by the sound that he rode his horse straight into the garden, starting a tradition of kings doing stupid things for love. When he spotted Mallika, she just stared at him. Suddenly feeling his exhaustion, he almost fell off his horse in an effort to properly greet her. Catching him in her arms (is this romantic or what?), she cradled him in her lap until he was able to muster the strength to get back on his horse.

Of course, they fell in love. Too mushy a setup not to fall head over heels.

Their marriage started out on a perfect note. He gave her enough servants to meet all her needs. She was, in turn, generous and kind. Both became followers of the Buddha, both became his friends. With a spunkiness that would make G.I. Jane proud, Mallika asked Buddha all sorts of questions about relationships. This was not a topic he had spent time on. Whenever he gave her an answer, she'd ask a second question, while everyone around her gasped at her impertinence. So what? The worst he could do was to respond with silence. Happily, he didn't. One time she asked Buddha why one woman was beautiful while another wasn't. His answer surprised her:

> The qualities and living conditions of people everywhere reflect the moral nature of their deeds in earlier lives. Beauty was caused by patience and gentleness, prosperity by generosity, and power by never envying others but rather by rejoicing in their success. Whichever of these

three virtues a person had cultivated would show up as
their "destiny" usually in some mixture of the three. [1]

Hearing him, Mallika vowed to be gentle and generous and to
never envy anyone. She gave alms to just about everyone who
came her way and built a huge ebony-lined hall for religious
conversations. She followed Buddha's instructions about being
a good wife and didn't even get jealous (!) when the king
brought a second wife home. When the other woman had a
son she rejoiced, and when the son was followed by a daughter
she was also openly pleased. Her behavior was such a model of
goodness that it led Buddha to do a teaching about women
where, to the shock of the monks, he said that if a woman was
clever, virtuous, well-behaved, and faithful, she was "superior
to a man."

But then the fights between the king and queen started.
And what fights they were. One time Queen Mallika was followed into her bathhouse by one of the palace dogs. "The dog
who lived in the palace had accompanied her there, saw the
queen bend down and started to perform an indecent act with
her. Though she took no active part; it was not a fitting thing.
However, since there are none who reject such gratification,
the queen endured the pleasure." [2]

The king, looking out one of the palace's upper-story windows, happened to see the incident and was horrified. Then
furious. Then enraged. When Mallika reentered the palace he
roared at her, "You despicable woman you deserve to be killed!
Why did you do such a thing?!" [3] Mallika feigned ignorance.
What was he talking about?! They had a huge, knock-down-
drag-out fight until she finally convinced him that he might
not have seen what he thought he did, shifting their fight from

a front-page story in the *National Inquirer* to an episode of *I Love Lucy:* "Your majesty, anyone looking down from up here on someone who goes to that bathhouse sees the image doubled. So it appears as if they were engaging in unseemly acts." [4]

Talking him into going down to the bathhouse himself, the queen went back upstairs to the window he was using and shouted down at him, "O foolish king, as king you have access to so many queens and yet you must engage in acts of dalliance with a she-goat? Does such an act befit a king?" [5]

Even though the king denied the behavior—since he really was alone—she persisted in haranguing him. Eventually the fight died down, but the fire of the relationship rage simmered. She lied, and some part of him knew it.

Their fights continued. Rage built until they almost came to blows over an argument about the duties of a queen. By this point they had stopped talking to each other, and when Buddha dropped by for a visit he asked about the absent queen. The king, still raging, said, "She has gone mad."

In reply, Buddha offered a way out of relationship rage. He talked about the value of perspective in a relationship. When we start to feel ourselves pulled into rage, we need to remember how much we care about the other person. We need to remember how human we both are and that everyone makes mistakes. We need to ask ourselves what Buddha or a wise woman would do in this situation and if we are willing to pay the karmic price for whatever retribution our mind is starting to consider. In Mallika's case, he reminded the king that he was the one who fell in love with her and made her queen so they could spend their lives together. How could they not reconcile? They had so many good years together. Behind all the melodrama they were both kind people. Was the king somehow forgetting how much he loved her? Mallika's "madness" had grown out of the situation the king had put her in.

Buddha then became silent and waited. Finally the king called for Mallika and they made up. They had both put too much work into their relationship to allow it to fall apart.

The peace didn't last. Before long another fight erupted, and for a while the king refused to even look at Mallika. As far as he was concerned her position as queen had gone to her head. Mallika's reaction? Relationship rage.

Again Buddha intervened. Rage has no place in relationships. They needed to remember their history and all the effort and energy both had invested in each other. Asking them to sit with him, Buddha told them a story from a shared former life, where they had both been heavenly beings. In that lifetime they had also loved each other deeply. One night a flood separated them, giving them a taste of what it would be like to be apart. The sheer shock of the separation caused them to vow to each other to stay together for a thousand years.

Moved, they reconciled. Mallika was so grateful to Buddha that she vowed to let go of her rage once and for all and to be a more skillful wife:

> With joy I heard your varied words,
> Which were spoken for our welfare;
> With your talk you dispelled my sorrow,
> May you live long, my ascetic, bringer of joy! [6]

This time the peace lasted for a long time. But relationship rage digs deep roots. Eventually they had another fight, one of those I-don't-care-if-you-are-king-I'm-going-home-to-my-mother fights. Again, Buddha, honorary marriage counselor, intervened. He told them another story, this one about how they were a married king and queen in an earlier lifetime. Only in that round, Pasenadi had become afflicted with leprosy. Forced to give up his crown, he went to live in a forest where he wouldn't be a burden to anyone, including his wife. Mallika had refused to let him go alone, following him, vowing to stay by his side, she cared for him with the gentleness of a mother caring for a sick baby. Her love was so strong, and care so constant, that the king fully recovered. Hearing the story, Pasenadi and Mallika begged each other's forgiveness and vowed to live in harmony and virtue.

This time they pulled it off, living together for many peaceful years by holding to a vision of a relationship where each person is honored and cared for and where patience and generosity provide the anchors needed to get through skirmishes. When Mallika died Pasenadi was beside himself with grief. Even Buddha's words couldn't console him. He had lost his best friend and lover. So attached was he to Mallika that he visited Buddha every day to ask about her. Could Buddha tell him where she is? Has she landed in heaven? After seven days Buddha could finally say, "Yes."

Pasenadi and Mallika learned to use perspective to put out the flames of their anger toward each other. How important is a moment of selfishness when someone has nursed you through leprosy in a past life? Perspective helps and perspective heals, and I suspect we've all had an opportunity to nurse each other through a hideous disease in a past life together.

Learning to See the Bigger Picture

I met my first real boyfriend at sixteen. Before that, dabbling: quick kisses to see if I could start and finish without getting my braces caught, quick kisses to see what someone else's mouth tasted like (french fries mostly). Unlike this N'Sync-morphing-into-Tori-Amos generation, I didn't have posters on my walls idolizing boy bands, not even the Rolling Stones—though to this day Mick Jagger has one of the sexiest mouths on the planet.

Having practiced kissing for two or three years, I never expected to have a proper boyfriend before, say, thirty. But at sixteen, on a train into Sydney, Australia, to spend a day in Hyde Park, there he was—the sexiest, scruffiest, I-wouldn't-trade-two-Brad-Pitts-for-him, red-headed, I'll-wear-a-winter-coat-in-the-middle-of-summer-if-I-want-to "Who" boy. (Who-boys were teens who purposely cut their hair to look like the members of the band the Who. This distinguished them from surfers and hippies and pure-form geeks. Well, maybe not all geeks, but most of them.) Red—I named him instantly—caught me gaping at him, baggie jeans, sandals, too big T-shirt, surfer-girl hair. By the time the train pulled into Sydney he was sitting next to me and we were comparing notes on everything from the best secondhand stores in Sydney to the cheapest fish-and-chip shops on the south shore. By the end of the day, I was writing his name inside hearts. Within three days, I was picking up our telephone on the half hour to make sure it was still working and yelling at my little sisters to limit their phone calls to three minutes if they valued their lives.

By the end of week two, Red and I were inseparable. I learned how to kiss real kisses, and he cleaned our swimming pool in the backyard so my father wouldn't throw him out of the house, since most of his meals were with us.

Even my sisters liked him.

We were a match made in heaven, and if I hadn't been so fairy-tale naive at the time, I'm sure we would have been lovers, but believe it or not, the kissing seemed to do the trick for both of us.

After three months together, I faced a tough school year, and he started looking for a real job, having completed technical school. We saw each other on weekends until, without warning, his phone calls stopped.

I was sure he had died.

Hysterical, I went looking for the body. Taking a day off from school, dressed in my boarding school blues, black Oxford shoes, straw hat, braids, and gloves, I took the train into Sydney where I found him at his desk—on the phone with another girl.

I was devastated. It had simply never occurred to me that our love would end, that our future wasn't sealed, that we weren't a match. His "I'm not good enough for you" fell on deaf, brokenhearted ears. I was sure I would die.

For months I mourned the loss of Red. I waited for him to come to his senses, to go back to school so he would be good enough for me, to show up on my doorstep begging forgiveness for not being the perfect prince. I couldn't eat or sleep for weeks and almost failed more classes than I care to count.

And I was mean. I yelled at everything and everyone. I could have burned the house down, scratched curse words onto the car, filled the swimming pool with lizard bodies. Furious mean. My sisters hid from me. Even my mother seemed to find different places to be when I growled my way home from school.

For six months I growled and fumed. Finally, chocolate and sanity restored me, but not before I owed everyone I knew,

025 NA 2ANA2N NNN 0 0124

〈No. 12A〉   74961

and at least a handful of complete strangers, huge apologies. After months of quiet contemplation, I was finally able to see a broader picture, that we were way too young, that he was right to tell me we weren't a long-term match. That my academic and athletic plates were way too crowded for a full-time boyfriend. That's when the rage left. That's when it finally skulked out my parent's back door.

Two years later I was in love again. The heart has such hope.

From a Place of Independence

Looking back at the dozen or so times I've fallen in and out of love in this lifetime, I've realized how correct the ancient women were to live lives that were not defined by love relationships. How much their own perspective of what needed tending—families, yes, but also their spiritual work—saved them from being consumed by relationship rage when the hard times hit them between the eyes. Romantic love comes and goes, like clouds. Sometimes soft and fluffy, sometimes stormy. Sometimes the clouds stick around for a while, but mostly they don't. Sooner or later they all leave.

Knowing this has taught me the value of independence. And how unproductive and even silly relationship rage is, since it is, inevitably, based on our own false expectations of what a relationship will be or do for us. We're bound to be hurt by our love relationships. It's part of the deal when we try to make permanent something that, by its very nature, isn't. Keeping a list of all the ways we've been wronged or hurt by our partner just makes us sick physically and emotionally.

Feeding our rage only harms. In 1999, the Templeton Foundation for Forgiveness Research in Richmond, Virginia, spent about $6 million to study how forgiving someone and moving on with our lives affects us. What happens if we simply let go of our rage? Some of their findings are amazing. In one study, more than seventy undergraduates at Hope College in Holland, Michigan, were instructed to cultivate vengeful thoughts for as little as sixteen seconds. The group experienced increased blood pressure, heart rate, and muscle tension. On the other hand, when they focused on forgiving, on just letting go, the stress indicators fell significantly.

In another study, the Atlanta Medical Center in Georgia found that HIV-positive patients who let go of their rage and forgave the person who passed on the disease to them—and forgave themselves for engaging in high-risk behavior—had stronger immune systems, and higher T-cell counts, than patients who couldn't. The Templeton Foundation also found that people who suffered from chronic anger had thicker blood due to higher red-blood-cell counts, putting them at an increased risk for stroke and heart problems. "We don't want to say that anger and lack of forgiveness are the only factors that can trigger cardiovascular problems, but they are definitely factors." [7]

Rage causes a stress response that can literally kill us. Our body releases hormones that accelerate our heart rate, blood pressure, and alertness, putting less essential functions such as digestion and our immune system on hold. If we can't let go of the rage, our bodies get stuck in stress mode. More and more, health practitioners are telling us that sustained rage or anger makes us incredibly vulnerable to anything from the common cold to heart disease. Best to drop it. Today, if you can.

Living our own lives, even in a relationship, offers protection from relationship rage. Knowing that all things are impermanent, that this is a truth of our lives, helps as well, because it locks us into having perspective. We've survived other heart-breaks. The sun will come up tomorrow. From a place of inde-pendence, where we define who we are, independent of who we are in love with, we can love without fear. When the rela-tionship ends, whether it comes from our partner dying or from the million other reasons why relationships end, we'll be okay. Heartbroken maybe, but not filled with rage. Not filled with a need to hurt.

In this place, where two people are honoring their best selves and where sometimes it makes sense to spend time together and sometimes it just doesn't, relationships can be partnerships. In this place we aren't threatened by a partner who needs space and time and other friends, because we do, too, and if things don't work out long term, that's okay as well, because we have learned more about ourselves through the mirror of our lover's eyes.

Perspective on what a relationship can really be teaches us which anchors really matter in our lives—for the ancient Buddhist women it was their spiritual work. And perspective heals because it reminds us that, in the end, relationships come and go and that the only thing you and I really have any con-trol over is our own behavior. And that being a shrew is not a winning choice. Perspective is what reminds us, even when we don't want to be reminded, that our clinging to "what ifs" and "if onlys" is a waste of time and that it would be a much better use of our time to just go help someone else—anyone else—scrub their bathroom or kitchen floors. At least then we'd have something to show for our time.

Over and over, Buddha taught the value of perspective. He reminded his followers ad nauseum that energy needs to go into our spiritual awakening, our practice. If we don't know

how much time we have left to fall into are own enlightenment—and we don't—how dare we spend hours, days, months,
or even years frivolously? Losing any of our precious life to
relationship rage is a complete waste of time, period. As they
began to understand impermanence and know the high costs
of rage, Buddha's female disciples put the bulk of their ener-
gies into their own spiritual growth, their own enlightenment.
What wisdom. Here's a bonus: When you and I have the
courage to put our own enlightenment first, all relationships
are joy. Why? Because in good times and bad they are feeding
us clues about the work we need to do. Here's where we might
be stuck, where we are setting impossible standards, where we
whine, where we blame our partner for all the wrongs of our
lives—past, present, and future. Here's where we are surpris-
ingly and wonderfully kind and compassionate and forgiving
and where we know how to giggle and dance and learn a new
theme song. Here's where we know how to be a refuge for
someone else's spiritual aches and pains, and here's where we
can offer a cup of tea held in both hands because we know, in
the end, that is really all we can offer someone else.

THE VALUE OF WOMEN FRIENDS
What if you are just plain stuck in rage? If it has locked you
into its seductive dance of righteous energy? What then? One
skillful response is to seek refuge in the wisdom of other
women. Ancient Buddhist women used each other as protection
against relationship rage. They used each other's patience, wisdom, and presence. When some of the women became known
as Buddha's surrogate teachers, the other women were able to
lean hard on them for help. Women ministering to women.

In Buddha's time the nuns cared for each other. Dhammadinna, one of the disciples Buddha singled out as excelling in expounding the dharma, was commonly referred to as a "good friend." Dhammadinna was married to a political and business leader before she became a follower of Buddha. When she became a nun, shortly after her husband announced that he was headed for celibacy and monkhood, she threw herself into her spiritual practice, isolating herself in the country until she experienced a profound awakening. Returning to her home-town of Rajagaha she found that her husband had decided to stay home after all. Seeing that something had changed in Dhammadinna, he asked her all sorts of questions. What was the deal with meditation? What does it feel like? How do you keep going? She told him that spiritual practice, and medita-tion in particular, consisted of focusing the heart, or paying attention and putting energy into one's effort. The way to cul-tivate spiritual understanding was to do one's spiritual work, to practice. When Buddha heard about their exchange he praised Dhammadinna, saying that he would have answered her hus-band's questions in the same way.

Dhammadinna became a great counselor to women. They came to her with their heartbreaks, their fears, their rage. She taught them to live their lives as their own and to be serious about their spiritual work. She coached and cajoled them to stop being so attached to pleasures that swiftly disappear:

> Eager for the end of suffering,
> full of awareness
> that's the way.
> When one's heart is not
> attached to pleasure, we say,
> that woman has entered the stream. [8]

Dhammadinna acted as a true north for women. They could go to her when they were lonely or scared or felt defeated by their circumstances. They could go to her when they found themselves attached to pleasure, obsessed with one of the monks or a former lover, or unable to make themselves let go of a relationship that was over or harmful to them. She healed them with her words and through her very presence.

Guidance from Other Women

This feels a little bit like going out on that limb, but I'll say it anyway: Having women ministers helps immeasurably in this relationship dharma realm. My experience is that men and women really do come from different planets. Maybe men obsess and worry and analyze relationships the way women do, but I've never seen it. Okay, maybe once or twice. But every single woman I have ever known has analyzed and fretted over her relationships.

This fretting and analyzing includes all the women ministers I know. Plus, we all have been in love at least once. So we understand, in our bones, what it feels like to be in love—sick love, healthy love, in-between love. We know what it is like to lie awake wondering if he or she will call, looking for clues that will tell us that our beloved cares about us. Also, most—maybe all—women ministers I know have had to live through, work through, falling out of love or being abandoned. When you talk to us and we nod, it is out of a shared experience. As a result, we can offer refuge and perspective.

In the mid-1980s I joined a small group of parents of teens with drug and/or alcohol problems who wanted to first understand and then help their children. As part of the preparation for joining the group I was asked to go through an intensive twelve-step program myself. Since there is a generous amount of alcoholism in this Irish-German American family I call home, I agreed to do it. The experience was intense (the most intense experience I'd ever had until I hit the seminary, which gave depth and meaning to the word). Anyway, at one point I was required to admit, out loud, things I had done to harm others, either willingly or unwillingly, and to clarify any amends I needed to make. At first I told myself, and the woman minister I had gone to, that there wasn't anything. (I so loved denial.) As I sat with the task, my heart spoke up. My husband and I were separated. According to me it was because he was a rager. The small print? I had also fallen in love with one of my business colleagues. But for that I probably would have been willing to go for one more round of relationship counseling. Saying these things out loud made me feel worse than shit.

The woman just nodded. "I know," she said. And I was sure she did. I talked about all the omissions, the judgments, the harsh demands I had put on the marriage. She just kept listening quietly, and nodding. She made me tea, kept refilling the cup without a word. I kept going for an hour and a half nonstop. Paraded through all the big emotions—sorrow, relief, rage, remorse. When I was finally empty she looked at me and said, "Let yourself be human. We all make mistakes. No woman I know has ever opened her eyes one morning and declared, 'Today I'll fall in love with someone who isn't my husband.' Women just don't do that."

I felt so comforted that I just sat in her kitchen and cried.

Remembering that day, what was so helpful was her obvious sharing of my emotions. She didn't just give me her blessing, she was saying, "Yup. Been there. Done that."

Women ministers know, firsthand, the ebb and flow of monthly cycles and how just because one day we are deliriously content doesn't mean that the day before our period we won't want a divorce. A woman minister can gently suggest that we might want to talk with our physician if we only seem to want a divorce on full moons. For myself, if a male minister ever suggested anything like that to me in my married days, I'm pretty sure I would have slashed his tires.

Women ministers matter because they know what it's like to serve different masters—family, work, self, community, spiritual yearning. When we talk about being too exhausted for sex because we're getting up each morning at four-thirty to drive a kid to swim practice, they get it. I'm not saying that men ministers don't. The issue here is simply the degrees of separation from the epicenter of emotional stress. Women ministers can often spot this particular brand of stress immediately—because it is theirs as well. To be effective ministers they've had to figure out how to manage the multiple roles themselves—so they'll at least be able to suggest to you what not to do. At best they can zero in on acupuncture points in your relationships and obligations, where letting off a little steam will be tremendously helpful and healing. As just one example, a minister friend of mine looked at me one day and said, "Organize a carpool for Jamie [my daughter]." I was running too hard, doing too many things to see my own exhaustion. "On the day you don't drive, stay in bed until you wake up on your own." I did and was surprised by what a difference one day made in my own energy level.

According to the U.S. Census Bureau, there are approximately 352,000 clergy in the United States, of which only about 14,200 are women. If I were you, I'd find one for the times when you'll need another woman's ear—one that can identify with the rage, the fear, the humiliation, and the yearning to move on. One who can offer perspective.

If there isn't a female minister within hearing distance, we can be healers for each other. In her book *Goddesses in Older Women: Archetypes in Women Over Fifty*, Jean Shinoda Bolen talks about how, for many of us, real friendships with other women don't happen until we're older. Too late I say. We need women friends sooner. In relationship suffering there are times when only a woman friend can help us to see clearly through our confusion and anger.

I can't imagine surviving the painful parts of a relationship without women friends. It was my friend Elizabeth who first suggested to me that the man I was with might have a "rage problem." No one else had red-flagged his behavior, even when they had witnessed it—not my mother, not my sisters, not my brother. Once she opened Pandora's box, Elizabeth, who was a witness to one rage, wouldn't let the issue die. She found a therapist for me to see, and I went because she was my friend, even though I was certain she was overreacting. Then, when a second therapist (I didn't trust the first one; she sounded so much like Elizabeth that I figured they were in cahoots—not that I'm paranoid in any way) bluntly told me to go to the bank, get $200, and then go home and pack my car with what I would need when I left, I realized that Elizabeth had given me both the courage and conviction to keep myself physically safe. Even after I found my own apartment, Elizabeth's presence prevented me from going back in those early-morning hours when I was able to convince myself that she and the therapists were wrong. My friend was my refuge even when my own rage—mostly at myself—later surfaced.

How could I have been so stupid, blind, you fill in the blanks.

Relationship rage can kill us if we let it. Left alone, it hardens into hate, and hate never heals. But when we soften the rage with perspective, by talking with friends or to ministers, it can be transformed—in its place, wisdom and fierce compassion. The world needs these things.

GRATITUDE PRACTICE

Finally, as crazy as this sounds, practicing gratitude can cut through relationship rage, à la Mallika and Pasenadi. I'm pretty skilled at getting angry. It happens fast, and it's hot. Almost always the anger comes from situations where someone has acted cruelly to another person. If the other person is a child, woman, or animal, my anger is rage. After thousands and thousands of hours of meditation and years of spiritual practice, much of it in temples, I have finally figured out how to transform the rage. Beyond the witnessing of it, finding something to be grateful for—anything, actually—cuts the rage. Gratitude that I'm alive, that spring always comes, that my behind hasn't sunk all the way to my knees, that my kids still love me. Gratitude keeps my emotions soft and opens up a space to choose compassion. In that space, the wisdom that a specific situation needs can also surface.

When I begin and end my days with gratitude it's like stashing warrior weapons for the next painful incident. I've gradually learned that it protects me at deep emotional levels. Up until two years ago I lived in an apartment facing a sweet little pond surrounded with beautiful landscaping. On the north side of the pond sits a small arched bridge like the ones you see in monasteries in the mountains of Korea. When I sat in the living room I could see the bridge out of the corner of my eye. One morning I noticed a young mother standing on it with two young children. They were leaning over the low railings, tossing crumbs to a handful of ducks. Suddenly the woman hit the taller child right across the face. I could hear the whack through my glass doors.

I jumped up from the couch and ran to the window just in time to see her hit him again, harder. I grabbed a loaf of bread and ran out the front door, furious. These were little kids. I was sure the little boy had welts on his cheeks by now. I ran around the front of the building until I got to the end of the bridge and then walked up to them, bread in hand. Handing the loaf to the boy, I turned to the mother, who looked shocked to see someone. Taking a deep breath, I started rambling about how frustrated I used to get with my kids when they were little, how they used to make me crazy, how hard it was to raise them on my own in the years when I did. Not looking at me, she nodded. We just stood there for a couple of minutes watching the boys throw crumbs at the ducks. Both kids were crying quietly. She was, too. Finally I asked her how I could help. She told me about her husband. How he was never home. Maybe he was having an affair. Maybe he was thinking of leaving her. She was so tired. Worried about money.

It turned out that there wasn't anything for me to do except witness her fear and exhaustion. I told her about the local women's center and some parenting classes that had helped me, and I played with the kids until the bread was gone. After they walked away I stood on the bridge heartbroken for all the parents in the world who are trying to raise children without skills or support. And I was grateful that the emotion filling me at that moment was compassion and not rage.

RAGE CAN BE LIKE a runaway horse, harming everything in its path. We need to make use of all the resources we can muster to transform rage into a different energy, one we can use to constructively get on with our lives. Beyond gratitude, for the sake of everyone we know, we need to be humble enough to ask for help if we get stuck in an enraged state and, when offered, accept it.

Chapter Four
JEALOUSY

I was in full possession of
body, speech and mind.
With the root of craving uprooted,
I have become cool and quenched.

—SUSAN MURCOTT, *The First Buddhist Women*

JEALOUSY DEFINED:
1. Jealous resentment against a rival, a person enjoying success or advantage, or against another's success or advantage itself.
2. Mental uneasiness from suspicion or fear of rivalry, unfaithfulness, as in love or aims.
3. Vigilance in maintaining or guarding something.
4. A jealous feeling, disposition, state of mind. [1]

Jealousy. Someone tries to take our lover away and, boom, there it is! Different from envy, where what we have just doesn't measure up to what someone else has, jealousy hits when something we have is threatened or lost to another person. The greater the threat, the bigger the jealousy.

It settles inside of us in stages. At first we have a feeling that something or someone is moving in on our partner. The more attractive, smart, and wealthy our competitor is, the more threatened we are. In the second stage, we start to obsess. We look for clues that something is going on. (She *did* touch his arm while they were talking.) Stage three? Our emotions kick in big time. Maybe we start feeling clingy even though we swore before every god we could name that that would never happen. Not us. Depression is a danger. We are hurt, angry . . . jealous. The monster has us by the ovaries.

Moving through jealousy is hard work because, at its worst, it makes us totally crazy. We can think of nothing else; we take obsession to new heights. We could kill. Sometimes we do. Crime statisticians estimate that as many as 35 percent of all murders are the actions of jealous lovers. Sometimes the murder takes the form of suicide. A friend of mine who is a therapist tells me that she can't get through a day without at least one client showing up consumed with jealousy. We want our lover, our mate, all to ourselves. And when we don't feel like we do, we're threatened down to our bones. And scared. And mad. A dangerous combination.

Left to its own devices, jealousy grows. Insecurity feeds it, as does any gap in our self-esteem. Maybe another woman has appeared on our daily landscape, a new colleague or classmate. My first real bout with jealousy was triggered by a next-door neighbor, a single woman, who started to show up just before dinnertime a couple of times a week. That she was attractive, smart, and funny made my "this could be a threat" antenna stand at full attention.

We find ourselves constantly assessing possible threats when we get stuck in jealousy. We analyze minutia. Does my husband chat with his female colleagues a little too long? Was he looking for an excuse to go over there? Is my partner staying at work longer and longer for no obvious reason? Is she taking longer to get dressed in the morning? And what's with the new lipstick? Sleep deteriorates because we're lying awake trying to figure things out, and the more sleep we lose, the worse things look.

Lodged in jealousy, our emotions run rampant. We're hurt but may not be able to explain why, since we have no proof of wrongdoing (yet). We're ashamed of ourselves. Maybe we become clingy, or feel rage. Maybe we become morbidly curious about the person threatening our relationship. Depression kicks in for many of us, as if just being jealous wasn't bad enough. In short, we're miserable. At that point all kinds of things can go wrong.

JEALOUSY IN BUDDHA'S TIME

In Buddha's day kings had many wives, a guaranteed haven for jealousy spores. Polygamy was regarded with some complacence as the customary right of kings and other powerful men. The criterion for its acceptance was whether a man could afford to keep more than one wife—that is, it was judged on practical rather than moral grounds. [2] Buddha's father, Suddhodana, had at least two wives, Buddha's mother, Maya, and his stepmother, her sister, Mahaprajapati. According to the history books, they got on just fine. I wonder.

The Consequences of Jealousy

King Udena of Vamsa lived in the capital city of Kosambi. He was not as lucky as Buddha's father was with his wives. When Udena is first introduced in Buddhist scripture he has two wives. Vasuladatta is a beautiful young woman he married both for her beauty and because he wanted to be politically connected to her family. Vasuladatta and the king had a rough-and-tumble beginning worthy of a Shakespeare play. Her father, King Candapajjota, had thrown Udena in prison, telling him he would be freed if he taught Candapajjota a magic mantra he was reputed to know. Udena refused at first. Eventually, however, the prison's conditions wore him down. Giving in, he made a deal with the king to teach the magic mantra to a hunchback in return for his freedom. Candapajjota agreed, dressing his daughter Vasuladatta as a hunchback because he didn't trust anyone else to tell him the mantra once it was learned. The king told Vasuladatta that she was going to learn a magic mantra from a leper, so she needed to be careful not to touch him. Then he put the two in a room with a curtain between them.

Udena started to teach the mantra. Things went well for a while until, one day, Vasuladatta just couldn't get it right. They started shouting at each other. "You good for nothing hunchback! Have you lost the use of your tongue or lips?! . . . You leper! Do you dare label someone like me a hunchback!" [3]

Furious, the young woman pulled back the curtain. They stared at each other, realizing that her father had set them up because he was afraid they would be attracted to each other.

And they were.

Immediately falling in love, they married. Rumor has it that their lust for each other was strong. (It must have been for their story to last 2,500 years.) And so was Vasuladatta's temper and Udena's arrogance. Soon after their marriage he met another beautiful and feisty woman, Magandiya. Like Vasuladatta, she was driven to be the main love of his life. As a result, Magandiya was jealous of anyone who came between her and the king. It was bad enough that she had Vasuladatta to contend with. When Udena fell in love with a third woman,

Magandiya's jealousy became too much to bear. At a business meeting with his finance minister, Ghosaka, Udena had met Ghosaka's adopted daughter, Samavati. In one sutra she is described as "quickly intelligent, with good practical sense." [4] She was so sweet and so free of guile that he immediately wanted her as his wife. As far as Udena was concerned she offered him what was missing from his first two wives, namely a loving and generous spirit.

The king sent a messenger to Ghosaka asking for his daughter's hand in marriage. The finance minister almost went crazy trying to decide how to respond to the king's request. On the one hand, Udena was known for his rages and Ghosaka didn't want to put his daughter in a position of being harmed. He also knew that Udena's existing wives would not welcome another wife in the harem. On the other hand, the king was the king, and his boss. He loved Samavati. After agonizing over his response, he finally sent a message to the king, refusing to hand over his daughter.

The king was so furious at Ghosaka's response that he had him thrown out of the kingdom. Samavati was not allowed to go with him. Seeing all that was going on, Samavati decided that she had to help her adopted father. She volunteered to marry the king. Udena was thrilled; Magandiya and Vasuladatta were not.

At the beginning, Samavati's life in the royal palace was okay, if a little tense. Her generous nature and spontaneous kindness made her a natural leader. When one of her servants, Khujjuttara, fell on her knees asking forgiveness for having stolen from Samavati, forgiveness was instant. Instead of punishing her, the young queen asked the servant what had caused her to steal so that she could remove the reason.

Khujjattara told her how she had heard the Buddha speak at the local florist shop. By the time he finished his teaching she had signed up as a disciple. The minute she made that commitment, she confessed, she wanted to admit any past wrongdoing. Samavati was so astonished by the change in her servant that she asked the woman to visit the Buddha every day and to bring his teachings back to the women's quarters so more people could receive his wisdom. This the servant did. Over time, the women's quarters became increasingly peaceful and Samavati more and more respected. Except by the first two wives, who were increasingly jealous of her popularity and growing power. They began to plot.

After hearing the teachings from her servant for a while, Samavati asked the king for permission to invite the Buddha to visit the palace himself. Receiving permission, she asked for a teaching. Buddha was committed elsewhere, but his attendant Ananda showed up. Ananda was such an effective teacher that Samavati had her own experience of enlightenment. She became so renowned for her kindness and compassion that even Buddha started referring to her as the woman lay disciple most skilled in spreading loving kindness.

Samavati's transformation made both Magandiya and Vasuladatta jealous beyond words. They decided that she had to go. Every day the king was falling more and more in love with her, spending more time in her quarters, ignoring them. Magandiya in particular had it in for Buddha as well. She was already spreading rumors that he and the monks were behaving inappropriately in other parts of the city when she decided that it was high time to get rid of Samavati. When her stories reached Ananda he was so put off that he wanted to leave the area completely, but Buddha talked him out of it. He promised that the monks' upright behavior would end the rumors eventually. They did.

Still, the two women plotted. Crazy with jealousy, they set traps for Samavati, trying to corner her in situations that would make the king angry with her. One time, knowing that she did not cook or eat meat, they had eight chickens delivered to the king with an anonymous note that recommended that Samavati should cook them for him. Although the king accepted her reasons for saying no, he was not happy with Samavati. Later, when Magandiya managed to instill rage in the king regarding Samavati, he was so upset by how easily manipulated he had been that he also went to Buddha for advice. You know the story already. Cooled down, he started visiting the women's quarters to hear Samavati teach, spending even more time with the young queen, ignoring the others.

Unable to stand such rejection, Magandiya decided to kill her rival. She set the entire women's palace on fire. Everyone inside, including the other queens, burned to death. King Udena went crazy when he heard of their deaths. That they were gone was unimaginable to him. When he realized that Magandiya had started the blaze, his punishment was that she and all her relatives be burned to death as well. Jealousy had destroyed all that was dear to him, leaving a kingdom of broken hearts in its wake.

We know jealousy can kill. Everyone I have ever asked knows at least one story about someone being killed because of jealousy. A second cousin killed his ex-wife's lover. A coworker put a contract out on her ex-husband. There is never a happy ending to manifested jealousy. Someone is always hurt.

And yet we get jealous. It helps to remember that jealousy is a "wantingness," a yearning that surfaces from not having someone we want. The incompleteness we feel makes us loony. The antidote is embarrassingly simple. We need to introduce other things into our lives that help us to feel more complete, more content. My vote, and the vote of the women in Buddha's life, is to kick spiritual practice into high gear. Pray more, sit more, read more, chant more. Scrub someone's kitchen floor, half as an act of kindness and half to release the ugly energy from your system. When we are filling the spaces in our days with these things, jealousy is transformed. We begin to experience flashes of okayness. In no time the feeling will grow into a deep contentedness if we continue with our spiritual work. Over time we forget what jealousy feels like and may even become grateful (yes, grateful) to the person who caused us to hunker down with our spiritual work.

Overcoming Jealous Anger

The story of Sirima and Uttara is another from Buddha's time that demonstrates the potency of jealousy. Uttara was the daughter of a wealthy merchant, Punna, in Rajagaha, a follower of Buddha. When word got out that she had reached the age of marriage, one of her father's friends, a merchant named Sumana, showed up to ask for her hand for his son. Punna frankly didn't think the son was good enough for his daughter and the offer was refused. Angry at his response, Sumana reminded the merchant that he had bailed him out of trouble many times when he was growing his business. Punna owed him.

Punna was pretty upset at this reaction. Finally he told Sumana that the problem was that both he and his daughter were followers of the Buddha. Since the son wasn't a follower there would surely be difficulties in the marriage. Sumana shrugged off his arguments and got all his buddies to lobby for the marriage. Finally, giving in to peer pressure, Punna said he'd let Uttara marry the young man.

Uttara was furious, but because she loved her father she gave the marriage her best shot. She cleaned, she cooked, she had sex. It didn't matter. She couldn't do anything right in her husband's eyes and became the scapegoat for her husband's entire extended family. After two and a half months she snuck back to her parents' house to beg them to let her come home: "Why have you thrown me into such a prison? It would have been better to have sold me as a slave than to have married me into a family of unbelievers." Her worst complaint? "In all the time I have been here I have not been allowed to perform a single deed of merit."[5]

Hearing her words, her father was so upset that he gave her money, fifteen thousand gold coins to be exact, so she could hire a courtesan to entertain her husband for two weeks while she did some spiritual practice. Finding the town's beautiful courtesan, Sirima, Uttara went off to perform meritorious deeds while her husband was preoccupied. To tell you the truth, as soon as Sirima showed up at his doorstep, her husband was pleased to have Uttara head out.

Uttara's first stop was the Buddha's resting place. Finding him there she begged him to visit her home on his daily begging rounds. He agreed. In addition, she started to show up for his teachings every day. By the end of the two-week period, Uttara had settled into a pattern of cooking for the monks every day as well as visiting with other spiritual seekers. Her husband, following her into the kitchen one afternoon, couldn't help but smile at her wackiness.

Here's where jealousy turns the scene ugly. Sirima happened

to look in the kitchen just as the husband was walking out. Seeing him smile, and knowing how much he liked sex, she figured that they had just had intercourse. Jealousy flew up her spine. She stormed into the kitchen and, seeing a cauldron of boiling oil in the corner, she scooped out a ladleful and turned toward Uttara. When Uttara saw her movement she instantly knew Sirima's intentions. Yet because she had been on a two-week intensive retreat with the Buddha, instead of anger, her mind was filled with thoughts of compassion: "My friend Sirima has done me a great service. The earth may be too small, the Brahma world too low, but my friend's virtue is great, for it is through her help that I have been enabled to make offerings and listen to the teachings. If now there is any anger in me let the oil burn me, but if I am free of anger it won't burn me." [6]

The oil, when it hit, felt like cool water. No damage was done.

This only made Sirima more jealous and more angry. She reached for a second ladle of oil, only to be grabbed by Uttara's maids, who were ready to beat her to a pulp, Buddhas teachings be damned. Shouting at them to stop, Uttara asked Sirima what was going on. Suddenly realizing what she had almost done, the courtesan burst into tears and begged Uttara for her forgiveness.

Uttara told her to ask Buddha for his forgiveness instead. The next day she did. And Buddha being Buddha used the story of the incident to give a teaching about overcoming jealous anger. We do it with nonanger. In the same way that evil begets anger, kindness begets kindness. We have to decide, moment by moment, how we are going to respond to the situations of our lives. Buddha was clear about the need for letting go of all of our negative emotions, even in the face of death.

It is possible to be in extremely difficult situations, such as when someone is clearly going after our mate, and to respond with nonanger. I've seen it. A young friend, Ronnie, realized that she was in sudden competition with her new husband's former wife for his heart. She responded with pure kindness. Even in the face of phone calls, even as she witnessed their interactions, she was kind. When I asked her about it Ronnie told me how bad she felt for the other woman. She had lost the love of her life, and now she was trying to raise a daughter on her own. All she really wanted was to be happy.

The key to nonanger is to stay focused on the other person. All she wants is to be happy. Made-for-television movies aside, in my experience, most women don't go after another woman's partner to hurt her. We are after the mate. In the throes of lust we tend not to consider anything or anyone else or the harm done. We're too blinded by our own hormonal thunderstorm.

As painful as the receiving end can be, once we realize that her actions are nothing personal, nonanger becomes possible. Its benefits are meaningful. Nonanger prevents us from doing or saying anything we might regret as soon as tomorrow. We don't create an enemy. Free of anger, we can see a situation clearly. Is this just someone else's problem, or is our mate responding? Are we overreacting or underreacting? Do we need to clarify or revisit the ground rules of our relationship?

THE EIGHTFOLD PATH

Many therapists tell us that there are two basic choices when we are feeling jealous. Either we can do what we need to do to "shore up the threatened relationship," or we can work on protecting our sense of self-worth. The Buddha offers a different take. He taught his followers that any heart-wrenching situation could be handled by what he called the eightfold path. Living a deeply moral life becomes a protective refuge from jealousy. This is about more than self-worth. And it is broader than simply shoring up a relationship. It is about living a life so full of kind and compassionate thoughts, words, and actions that jealousy doesn't stand a chance.

Right Understanding: Seeing life as it is.

When we see our life as it is, the factors that lead to jealousy become painfully clear. We may see how we started to ignore our mate or when we started to notice that our cousin's marriage seemed happier than our own. We can see where we started to obsess and where we started to make room for our growing discomfort instead of addressing it. With the clarity comes the possibility of shifting, of seeing where we can make changes so jealousy is no longer a part of our lives.

For example, we think we see our lives clearly, you and I. But we don't. Life is tough. We fight this truth with everything we've got, figuring that a new thinness, different colored hair, or a nose job will make us more attractive to potential mates, or to our existing one. Then we'll be happy. Or a higher paying job will make us happier. What we often don't realize is that even if we find a compatible mate or that perfect job, life will continue to be difficult because we will still want things we don't have or not want things we do have. Understanding these dynamics forces us to look at the real themes of our lives, such as times when we are genuinely content and times when we are not. We'll be forced to see when we're feeling secure in a relationship and when we're just pretending.

Right Thought: Having a pure mind; avoiding feelings that obstruct progress to perfection "such as lust, malice or cruelty." [7]

Jealousy is fed by thinking. It is impossible to be jealous if our minds aren't feeding us ammunition, the hundred reasons why we have every right to be jealous. These thoughts are mental junk mail. Right thought is about clearing them out and replacing them with kindness or spaciousness. A simple way to do this is simply to repeat the mantra "It's okay" every time a jealous thought starts to form. It may take a while, but sooner or later our minds will start to let go of the negative thinking and start heading in a more positive direction.

Right Speech: "Cultivating the same characteristics in one's words as one's thoughts. One should refrain from telling lies, backbiting, idle gossip and the like, and address people in a kindly and tolerant manner. Correct speech should not be loud, excited or opinionated; it should also avoid inflaming the passions of others. . . ." [8]

Jealousy makes fishwives out of every one of us. We talk too loud, even screech. We curse. Our sounds are ugly. Sometimes simply speaking softly can take the edge off our jealousy. Sometimes the right speech is no speech. Refusing to say anything out loud that we could not say in front of the Dalai Lama or our mothers also helps. Right speech is difficult when we want to lash out at the world. At the same time, it is a great shield, protecting us for later when calm has made its way back into our days. It is excruciatingly painful to be reminded of the viciousness that came forth from our mouths in a jealous tantrum. Better to bite a hole in our cheek. Better to get our tongue pierced so it hurts too much to say anything. We'll be grateful for the silence later. So will everyone we know.

Right Action: Right action is basically made up of five Buddhist precepts. "The first of these 'five commandments' prohibits killing and urges charity and kindness to all living things. The other precepts deal with theft and generosity; sensuality; sincerity and honesty; and the use of intoxicating drink or drugs." [9]

Here's what I know about jealousy and right action. In the throes of jealousy, it is best to do nothing. Your body has been invaded by a green-eyed monster. He only wants to harm. If you force yourself to just be with the jealousy (make your best friend sit on you if you have to), what will happen is this: You will cry. Yet in the crying is a great release and a path out of the jealousy.

Right Livelihood: "In earning your living you should not engage in business or activity that conflicts with or compromises the conduct of life according to Buddha . . . any kind of deceit or exploitation, anything that causes harm or injustice to others is to be avoided." [10]

Working at a job that feeds our best selves helps to protect us from jealousy. When we are nurtured we feel fulfilled, happy, content. We may feel pangs of jealousy given certain situations, such as having a crush on a boss who is dating someone else, but we have so much else going on for us that there isn't time to give in to the obsessing that grows jealousy.

Right Effort: "Fostering noble qualities . . ." [11]

We're lazy, you and I. We don't mean to be, but we are. The older I get, the more convinced I am that it is either (a) human nature, or (b) we're all eating too much sugar and it's slowing us down. At any rate, throwing ourselves into whatever we are doing is right effort. The surprise reward is that it brings a sense of well-being and makes whatever we're doing fun. This includes scrubbing kitchen floors the old-fashioned way—on our hands and knees.

Right Mindfulness: "The development of intellectual awareness in the service of spiritual progress . . . in simple terms this means training one's mind to examine things in such a way as to recognize what is important and not to be led astray . . ." [12]

There is a wonderful Zen story about a woman who climbs several mountains to find a Zen master known for his wisdom. After years of searching she finally tracks him down. She makes him offerings of fruit and incense and asks for instruction. "Pay attention," he says.

"Is there anything else?"

"Pay attention."

"Is that it?!"

"Yes."

It's true. When we pay attention we can cut jealousy off at the first sign that it is about to move in on our body-mind. I can tell when jealousy is about to show up, because the frown line on my forehead deepens and a feeling of crankiness takes over my brain. My whole body tenses up and even feels a little feverish. Mostly the discomfort passes. But if any of the sensations hold I know to call one of my friends to remind me to let go or to sit in meditation or do some manual work. I cannot tell you how wonderful it is to feel jealousy come and go like a miniature internal rainstorm rather than lose any precious time to feelings that are only destructive.

Right Concentration: "The practice of meditation that leads to a full understanding of the impermanence of things and eventually to Nirvana." [13]

Right concentration is about sticking with our mindfulness. Concentration provides the energy and focus we need to stick with what is right in front of us rather than imagine future catastrophes or relive past ones. It keeps us grounded, which is deeply comforting.

MINDFULNESS

When we can see that our suffering is coming from a craving for something we don't have (i.e., a secure relationship), we can then start to address the jealousy. For difficult emotional situations, Buddha would instruct his followers to be mindful, to pay intimate attention to what they were experiencing, what their senses were up to, so they could see what they needed to do to get through the situation.

Good medicine, mindfulness is about paying attention to what is right smack in front of us. It is a spiritual practice as well as a realistic method for reducing stress. Mindfulness means slowing down and breathing deeply and noticing your surroundings, as opposed to living your life as though you're looking out of the window of a fast-moving bus. When I am being mindful I notice that the seat of my chair has a black vinyl cushion and the floor is hardwood. I notice how the owners of the coffee shop where I'm sitting matched the table-tops to the floor and how they take time to keep their plants healthy. I notice that the shape of the cup I'm holding is more square than round, that I can't quite call it yellow because there's a little brown in it. In mindfulness I notice that the wall beside me has little nails sticking out of it—maybe to hang pictures—that the shop's "OPEN" sign is actually blue and red, not purple like someone told me. I can feel my heart beating and the shape of my favorite black Pilot Precise pen. In this place, paying attention to all of my senses protects me from getting caught up in negative emotions. There's no room. Instead, I get to watch my emotions come and go, come and go. In a place of mindfulness I can zoom in on right now instead of getting too caught up in yesterday or tomorrow. The feeling is sweet. Comforting. A refuge.

In this place of true attention, it is impossible to lie to ourselves. What we feel is what we feel. As one result, the light of true attention makes for constant little miracles because it somehow breaks big chunks of emotions into bite-sized pieces we can ingest and digest—and jealousy is one of those emotions. Without mindfulness, jealousy tends to be big, dark sludge. It makes us tired, miserable, hate-filled. And it is sticky, so when we get caught up in jealousy it is tough to get uncaught. Instead, we sink deeper and deeper as it hardens, until something explodes. The explosion further fuels our righteousness and misery. Giving into it makes us feel worse about ourselves, and even after we brush ourselves off after an explosion that will cost at least some karma, there jealousy is, staring at us, daring us to try something else.

Mindfulness breaks the pattern. Why? Because with mindfulness we can see that our jealousy is really made up of lots of other emotions—fear, anger, hurt, sadness, loneliness, embarrassment. Once we see the other emotions we can work with them individually until jealousy becomes a small thorn in our side instead of an emotional fever come to run us over.

When my son's father and I parted ways it wasn't because one of us had committed any heinous relationship-ripping crime. We had moved from Oregon to the University of Michigan together to get our doctorates. And because I was a city-loving woman and he was a mountain man, we agreed to live in Ann Arbor until we both finished our graduate course-work and then we'd move to a place where he could be in the mountains within a couple of hours at the most and I could get the *New York Times* on Sunday. In those days, Portland, Oregon, didn't get the *Times*.

By the end of our first semester my husband was ready to head back to the Northwest. The University of Michigan was unbearably competitive, and it didn't help when another student in the program stole a major paper my husband had written and handed it in under his name. By the first thaw he was at the end of his rope. Was I going with him?

Terrified that I would end up isolated in the mountains making quilts, I refused. Worse, I felt betrayed. We had made a deal.

Brokenhearted, we separated. I stayed in Ann Arbor. As long as we were both single we stayed close. We talked on the phone, visited. He helped me find an apartment. I was fine when he had the obligatory affair with a much younger woman. When my Portland friends called in to report it, they described her as a younger version of me. I knew her. Since she was smart and beautiful, and he and I were still in contact quite a bit, I was (mostly) happy for him. But their affair ended, and after a few more short flings he fell in love. Hard. This time it was with a drop-dead gorgeous newscaster—funny, smart, sexy. Did I say thin?

I was jealous. I was stay-up-all-night-and-obsess-about-it jealous. Do-my-best-not-to-wish-her-ill-but-check-the-news-on-the-chance-she-might-be-gone jealous. Even hearing her name riled me. And when I called his house in the mornings (I know, I know . . .), and she answered the phone, my brain went ballistic.

Until she invited me to lunch when I was visiting Portland.

Shocked and, okay, curious, I went. The restaurant was a beautiful garden café, and she was equal to the place. Without waiting for us to order she told me she'd like to be my friend. Said she could feel a tension from me (no kidding) and wanted to make sure I was okay with their relationship. Stunned, I found myself liking her and even hoping that their relationship would work out.

That afternoon, though, jealousy reared its predictably ugly head.

This time I sat with it mindfully, motivated to get rid of it. Instead of just labeling what I was feeling—jealousy—I watched to see what was really there and found a bouquet of emotions. First, I was ashamed of myself for giving up a good man for what increasingly felt like a frivolous reason. I felt dowdy compared to the newswoman—and boring. Stupid, even. Watching the emotions come and go for a while, I realized that if I paid attention to them without dwelling on them, they came and went like waves on an ocean. Here one second. Then gone. And they changed shape, got smaller.

After awhile it became clear that what I had been calling jealousy was really sadness. And that I just needed to be sad—that I still had plenty to offer a relationship. After only a week of mindfulness practice regarding my reaction to the lunch, I decided that while I couldn't be her friend, I could honestly wish the two of them happiness and move on. So I did.

DECIDING WHAT REALLY MATTERS

In addition to mindfulness, reframing the things that matter in our lives helps us to move past jealousy. Years ago I worked as a management consultant. Early on I became involved with the business plan for a women's magazine. It was a great project. I loved the client. The problem was that the start-up costs of the magazine were so high that I just couldn't make the numbers work. I couldn't figure out how the client could ever make any money. She was furious. I was miserable. I lost her to another firm that apparently could figure out a way for her to make money. Then I was miserable and jealous. After losing an entire day to self-flagellation I called an older woman, someone who had been a partner in the firm for years. Her advice was blunt.

"Did you do the best you could?"

"Yes."

"Did you apologize for any unskillfulness or mistakes?"

"Yes."

"Will this matter in five years?"

"No."

"Then stop thinking about it."

Relative to everything else in my life, the loss of the client was a disappointment, but that was all. It wasn't like hearing that my child had been harmed, or my parents.

Reframing. Last night I spent some time sitting with a young woman dying from complications related to AIDS. She's in her early twenties—tall, athletic, went to Ivy League schools. She got the disease from a man who raped her at the age of nine. She may not make it to next Christmas. Right now all she wants is enough energy to make it through two art classes so she can die without any loose ends.

What really matters in our lives?

Jealousy is self-indulgent. It gives us something to obsess about, and with that obsession it gives meaning in our lives— we have a relationship to defend. Yes, an enemy is at the gate, but too many of us take jealousy to heights that only waste hours, days, months, even years in lives that are already too short.

Here's some crazy wisdom: Just drop it.

The women who followed Buddha were keenly aware of the preciousness of each moment of their lives. As a result, they closely monitored their thinking so they could focus on what mattered the most—their own spiritual growth. Everything else was dropped, even jealousy. If they started to get caught up in any negative emotions, Buddha or one of his disciples was available to remind them to "hurry, hurry" to do their spiritual practice. No one else could do the work for them and, relative to their spiritual work, everything else in their lives, including relationships, was secondary. Only their spiritual efforts would benefit them to their death and beyond. Everything else ended. Who knew when they would ever have another chance to become enlightened, to live a life free of emotional suffering? That was where their energy needed to be focused.

When we reframe what matters in our lives it is relatively easy to let go of jealousy. A woman who goes to a different church told me about how she was consumed with jealousy as a result of an affair her husband had. Until she found out she had breast cancer. Then the jealousy immediately disappeared as she shifted her focus to getting well. She joined a support group to help her "spit my jealousy out," and she discovered new interests, including Buddhism, medieval art, and vegan cooking. At the same church, a younger woman left a young marriage because jealousy was such a destructive component of the relationship. Deciding to throw herself into her religion instead and getting involved in peace work healed her broken heart.

When we are able to be "our own spiritual lamp," to better control how we expend our energy, the positive results are wondrous. I can't remember the last time I was jealous of anything or anybody. This is not because I am better than anyone else, since that is untrue. It is because I spend so many waking hours meditating and being mindful. Even as I stumble, negative emotions fall away almost immediately, or if they do pop up, they come and go quickly. Sometimes I think I'm the only woman in America who is honestly pleased for everyone who has a Valentine on Valentine's Day even when I don't. While they are all out at dinner, I get the gym to myself. A small but meaningful miracle to someone who spends most of her gym time on machines nobody else wants to use.

Having role models helps a lot here. They act as reminders that there is a better us inside the green-eyed monster who is wearing our name. Samavati continues to teach us about steering clear of jealousy. Even before her run-ins with Magandiya, her life was filled with interests other than relationships. When she was small, a plague hit her village, and only her family survived. To protect her, Samavati's father took her to Ghosaka. Because she had gone through so much, even as a young woman, Samavati had a balanced view of relationships; she was incapable of feeling jealousy. Instead, she spent her days helping to distribute food to the poor, setting up distribution systems that would make the king's efforts more efficient. Because of her capacity for mindfulness, for paying attention to what is right in front of her, her life was full. She was genuinely happy for the king's other wives when he chose to spend time with them. Her happiness was a shield jealousy couldn't penetrate. The same thing is true for us. When we are genuinely happy for someone else it is impossible to be jealous. Try it.

FORGET JEALOUSY. Instead, practice being genuinely happy for the good fortune of everyone else. When our friends fall in love, let's be happy for them. When our sisters do, ditto. And let's practice all year so next Valentine's Day I won't be the only one working out at the gym, unfazed by a life unmated.

Chapter Five

OUTSMARTING THE PULL OF AN AFFAIR

Four kinds of misfortune come
to those who commit adultery:
Bad karma,
disturbed sleep, and
a bad reputation
are already known.
There is also the risk
of being reborn in hell.

Trading bad karma
and bad destiny
for the brief joy of adultery
brings heavy punishment.
Don't consort with
someone else's partner.

—*The Still Point Dhammapada*

AN OLD BUDDHIST STORY: Once upon a time there was a woman with a strong streak of jealousy who lived with her roving-eyed husband in Savatthi. Unfortunately, she had good reason to be jealous, because her husband was having an affair with one of their maids. When the woman found out, she was so furious that she cut off the maid's ears and nose. The maid, in turn, was so furious that she went to the Buddha to find out how she might revenge the woman.

Instead, the Buddha told the maid that she was harming the woman. Just because we don't know that we are "doing evil" doesn't let us off the karmic hook. An evil deed, even when done in secret, will ultimately cause great pain and unhappiness, especially to the evil-doer. Like losing our ears and noses.

ANCIENT INDIA'S WOMEN

Before Buddha's time, the status of women in India wasn't great. Daughters were sources of great anxiety to their parents. On the one hand there was the terror that they might not be able to marry her off. On the other was the fear that, if she did marry, they would be financially ruined by the costs of the wedding festivities. Once married, cultural norms called for complete subservience to the husband—and his family. Since most women were married between the ages of sixteen and twenty, they were easily bullied and often made the family scapegoat. If anything went wrong, they were blamed.

When Buddha began to teach, the status of women changed. They were given more equality and were better respected, even though all wives were not created equal. There were actually ten types of wives: "those bought for money, those living together voluntarily, those who are to be enjoyed or made use of occasionally, those who have given cloth, those who have the quality of providing the house with (a bowl of) water, those who have put up a head-cushion (in order to carry vessels on their head), those who are slaves and wives, those who are artisans and wives, those who are flag-brought, and those who are temporary or momentary wives." [1] Whatever the type, for the first time wives were able to make their own decisions about how they would live their lives—as servants or partners of their husbands. Although they were confined to mostly domestic activities, they were more openly spiritual and social than ever before.

There was even more freedom to choose a husband. The princess Kanha, for example, talked her mother into convincing her father to hold an assembly of available men so she could choose a husband. Women were also free not to marry and were no longer obligated to marry simply to save their family's reputation. At the same time, the women who did choose to marry took more and more authority in running homes and, in matters both temporal and spiritual, were increasingly regarded as their husbands' equal and worthy of respect. As mothers they were definitely honored and revered. In fact, as mothers, their positions were unassailable. A woman was no longer regarded so much as a part of her husband, so completely his possession, that when bereft of him her life virtually ceased. This was a huge shift.

With increasing autonomy and respect came other problems, like love affairs. The general practice of marriage was monogamy, in spite of the kings' and wealthy merchants' penchant for multiple wives. Women were expected to be completely loyal to their spouse, whatever style wife they were. They were also expected to be loyal to those dear to their spouses, to care for them, to make sure that they were not harmed by scandal. Complete devotion was considered the most honored behavior.

A Model Wife
King Pasenadi's wife, Mallika, in her later years, was held up as the official benchmark of what complete devotion means. She

cared for, and even loved, his other wives. She spent time with him when he wanted to be near her and literally moved out of his quarters when he needed space or time with someone else. She took care of their son, Ajatasattu, his extended family, and his servants in sickness and in health.

When Ajatasattu came of age, he didn't want to wait for his father to die to become king. When a scandal surfaced regarding an unskillful legal decision Pasenadi had made, the prince used it as an excuse to throw his father in jail. His mother, terrified that the king would starve to death in prison, schemed to smuggle food to him. First she smuggled food through the gates in a golden bowl. When she was caught she started to hide food in the flap of her gown. When guards found that, she hid food in her headdress. When that food was discovered, she hid food in her shoes. By then the guards knew to check all of her clothing. So she started to bathe in heavily scented water and then, clean, covered her body with honey for her husband. It kept him alive until her son found out what she was doing. Furious, he refused to let her see the king at all after that. The king died of starvation.

Her demonstration of devotion was frequently used as an example of the ideal behavior of a wife. When someone asked Buddha if Pasenadi's wife's behavior was really the appropriate model, Buddha said that a wife who possesses five things—beauty, wealth, a supportive extended family, the ability to have children, and virtue—was a model wife. She had all five.

At the other extreme, the most harmful thing a woman could do in a marriage was to emotionally stray. Buddha continually warned his followers about the dangers associated with lust, particularly when that lust was aimed at an inappropriate person. If you feel attracted to someone you know you shouldn't be attracted to, immediately picturing them as a family member—a mother or father, a sister or brother, a daughter or son—could help stem the tide of lust. As far as Buddha was concerned, any inappropriate sexual liaison was one of the activities guaranteed to bring a person to ruin:

> Slaughter of life, theft, lying, adultery—
> To these no word of praise the wise award . . .
> Let the wise [person] avoid an unchaste life
> as a burning heap of coals;
> not being able to live a life of chastity,
> let him not (transgress with another's
> spouse). [2]

DEVOTION

Mallika's story demonstrates the value of cherishing our mate. When we can hold in our hearts how precious this person is, even as she snores through the night, we can perform miracles in honor of our love. Maybe we won't cover our bodies in honey, but we will look for other ways to care for this person we hold dear. Maybe it means that we'll take the time to buy fresh organic vegetables to cook rather than an instant stir-fry. Or we'll make a vow to keep as much vegetable juice in the refrigerator as Coca-Cola. Clean cotton sheets instead of slightly-rank-because-it's-been-over-a-week-since-they-were-changed sheets. Maybe we'll go for a walk when we get home from work instead of filling the air with a litany of the day's frustrations. Taken singly, these actions are little things. Writ large, they are a love poem.

Beauty goes. Wealth can go. Who knows where our families are headed? More and more of us question having children in a world weighed down by overpopulation. But virtue in the form of devotion never grows obsolete. It is a sweet nectar, capable of feeding the fire of love in miraculous ways.

Our acts of devotion keep our mates alive in our hearts. They remind us why and how we fell in love in the first place. They keep our love fresh. Small constant reminders protect us from the pull of an affair as well. When we put so much energy into caring for someone who is precious to us, we find we don't have any left for another. Devotion is a warrior woman's shield, saving marriages and protecting families day by day.

Sexual Attraction

Then as now the pull of sex was strong. Vimala was a beautiful young prostitute who, on seeing the monk Moggallana, decided that he had to be hers. Vimala was a young woman accustomed to using her sexuality to get whatever she needed or wanted. Proud of it, she used seduction as a way to control men. She called herself a "hunter" who spread her "snare" for fools. Rejection was not part of her life experience. Then along came Moggallana—a celibate monk, one of Buddha's top two disciples. Talk about a challenge.

When she was finally able to meet with him face-to-face, it was all she could do not to faint from the sexual tension she felt. Vimala became so obsessed with Moggallana that she followed him for days, even going to where he was staying and waiting outside, hoping for a glimpse of him. She did everything she knew how to do to seduce him: she flirted, she wore seductive clothes, seductive smells, whispered seductive words. All she could think of was how wonderful it would be to have an affair with him. That he was a monk meant nothing to her.

While Moggallana did his best to be patient, one day he had it. And his words to her weren't pretty: "You bag of dung, tied up with string. You demoness with lumps on your breast. The nine streams in your body flow all the time, are vile smelling, and full of dung. A monk desiring purity avoids you as one avoids dung." [3]

Vimala was flabbergasted. Having spent a lifetime surrounded by or participating in love affairs and sex for pay, it never occurred to her that someone would reject her. She was young, smart, and beautiful. Men literally stood in line for her.

The vileness of Moggallana's words stung her silent. She was shocked enough to seriously consider his words. His ability to reject her so out of hand meant that he had found something that mattered to him more than sex. What it was she couldn't imagine. But she was curious enough to find out about it. Vimala ended up asking for instruction from the Buddha. She was determined to learn what the mendicant life offered that had such power over sensual pleasure, over inappropriate liaisons. To do this, she decided to completely let go of the life she knew. She gave up sex and became a nun. In her own renunciation, she found a deep spring of happiness and, ultimately, enlightenment:

> Young,
> intoxicated by my own
> lovely skin,
> my figure,
> my gorgeous looks,
> and fame too,
> I despised other women.

Dressed to kill
at the whorehouse door,
I was a hunter
and spread my snare for fools.

And when I stripped for them
I was the woman of their dreams;
I laughed as I teased them.

Today,
head shaved,
robed,
alms wanderer,
I, my same self,
sit at the tree's foot;
no thought.

All ties
untied,
I have cut
men and gods
out of my life,
I have quenched the fires. [4]

Sex is a strong drug. When we're in the throes of a sex-driven relationship, or are used to using sex as a weapon, it is hard to believe that there is a better life out there. The thing is, sex always ends, and even great sex gets old. Then what do we do? Moggallana was a great friend to Vimala. He forced her, literally, to look for a deeper source of satisfaction, a permanent source of happiness. She found it in spiritual work.

Sooner or later we will have our last sexual encounter. Maybe it will happen at forty-eight. Maybe at sixty. Then what? Acknowledging that sex will come to an end is a powerful incentive for looking at our lives through a different lens, one where there is no sex. We'll see the possibility of different forms of love in our friendships, in our concern for the planet, in our connections with animals. Just looking through the lens will show us where there is work that needs doing. For most of us it is our spiritual work. We need to take measures, you and I, for when that day hits, if it hasn't already. We need to offer up some part of our day for self-nurturing—reading, art, studying, prayer, meditation. Ironically, the more we do outside of sex the more interesting we become to our partners, because we are a mystery that continues to unfold. You'll see.

Your Spiritual Path as a Refuge

While Vimala was able to walk into the sunset, free of sexual yearning, Nanda Gotama, Buddha's stepbrother, had a tougher time. When Buddha returned home to visit his stepmother, father, wife, son, and cousins several years after his enlightenment, a handful of them were so swept up in his words that they demanded to be accepted as followers then and there. His stepbrother Nanda was in this group. Though his intentions were pure, he couldn't get the image of his beautiful wife out of his head. In the forest, he saw her image. On the paths where they walked, he saw her image. He couldn't eat or sleep he was so obsessed. Finally, in agony, he went to Buddha for help:

> Reverend Sir, when I left my house my noble wife,
> Janapada-Kalyani with her hair half combed, took leave

of me saying, "Noble sir, please return immediately."
Reverend sir, it is because I keep remembering her that
I am dissatisfied with the religious life that I am now living; that I cannot endure to live the religious life any
longer; that I intend to abandon the higher precepts and
return to the lower life, the life of a lay man. [5]

When Buddha responded, even trying to bribe him with
visions of beautiful women in his next life, Nanda couldn't get
past the pull and went home. His sister, also named Nanda,
decided that she wanted to be a follower of Buddha as well. So
graceful and beautiful that she was called Sundari-Nanda,
"beautiful Nanda," the young woman had the same problems
with lust that her brother had. Her thoughts were always filled
with sensual pleasure. She loved being attractive and flirting.
She loved being near all the monks, because many of them
were good-looking. She was afraid that, like Nanda, she would
give in to lust, and wasn't sure she was ready for the rigorous
life of a nun.

Seeing her, Buddha decided to gather all the nuns together
to "receive instructions." Nanda actually hid from him, sure he
was going to talk to them about letting go of desire. Unfortunately for her, he named her specifically when he called the
group together. Nervously, she waited to hear what he had to
say. But he surprised her. Instead of saying anything, he con-
jured up a vision of a woman even more beautiful than
Sundari-Nanda. In that instant he had her full attention. Then
he made the vision visibly age right in front of the group of
nuns. In the space of a less than an hour the women got to see
the budding of beauty and then its decay and death.

Everything is impermanent. Even beauty. Even affairs.

Buddha specifically asked his half sister to think really hard about how the body deteriorates and ages and how we need to protect ourselves from distractions that are always impermanent.

> Nanda, behold this body,
> Ailing, impure and putrid,
> Develop the meditation on the foul,
> Make the mind unified, well composed. [6]

As only a little sister who adores her older brother can, Nanda swore to take her spiritual practice more seriously. She promised to let go of her clinging to her looks and to stop fantasizing about the monks. Nanda proceeded to meditate "unwearying by day and night." She was so energetic and vigilant with her practice that Buddha later praised her as the foremost among nuns who practiced meditation. Completely letting go of desire, she became his true spiritual heir:

> "As is this, so was that.
> As is that, so this will be,
> Putrid, exhaling a foul odor,
> A thing in which fools find delight."

> Inspecting it as it is,
> Unwearying by day and night,
> With my own wisdom I pierced right through
> And then I saw for myself.

> As I dwelt ever heedful,
> Dissecting it with methodical thought,

I saw this body as it really is
Both inside and outside too.

Then I became disenchanted with the body,
My inward attachment faded away.
Being diligent and detached at heart
I live at peace, fully quenched. [7]

Meditating on impermanence, on the fleetingness of beauty and on the foulness of bodies drove Nanda into a spiritual awakening—a realm light-years away from the world of affairs. She realized that spiritual happiness was permanent, whereas body-driven happiness was fleeting. In enlightenment, the shape, size, age, and health of our bodies is irrelevant.

THE IMPERMANENCE OF BEAUTY

We won't always be young. We won't always be pretty. Sooner or later the whole world will start calling us "ma'am" and may even stop seeing us altogether. Everything is impermanent. This includes all the attributes that make us sexy and most of the things—at least the physical ones—that ignite sexual relationships. We need to remember this so we can stop clinging to impermanence. In the morning we shout, "Impermanence surrounds us!" at the abbey as a reminder not to cling. For a year I used the word *Impermanence* as a screen saver so I could see where I was clinging.

We won't always be alive. We won't always be young. Remembering this, thinking about it, helps to put every single thing in life into perspective. We love our partner, but since everything is impermanent he won't always be in our lives. Knowing this helps us to see our time together as precious.

We are young. Everything is impermanent. Thinking about this, we take time to enjoy our energy, to travel and explore, to be careful not to settle too early with a permanent mate and children. The size-eight dress fits today, but it won't always fit. Instead of buying more dresses, we wear it more often, loving how it feels, appreciating it now.

Thinking about impermanence helps us to let go of what doesn't matter and to deeply appreciate what we do have—a body that functions, a plant blooming in the yard, our cat. Appreciation, in turn, has a way of morphing into a sweet contentedness where the pull of affairs weakens, especially the damaging ones.

THE DAMAGE OF AN AFFAIR

Adultery, having an affair with someone who isn't our partner, constitutes one of the all-time, hell-inducing inappropriate sexual relationships we can get our sweet selves into. Adultery spoils a relationship, period. It spoils it because it represents a broken promise in a world of broken promises, the promise to be sexually faithful. It spoils a relationship because it is a deception of the deepest kind. Adulterers deceive their mates by pretending they have feelings they don't have. They lie. Even in their silence sit lies. Having an affair when we are married or committed puts us in the position of living a secret life. While we are pretending to live one life, we are actually living two. And the one with our committed mate doesn't have a chance when it has to compete with the fantasy of an affair in which the time spent with the other person is filled with the best version of ourselves. These are the times when our legs are shaved and our underwear is new. We are free of the responsibilities of everyday life, where the coffee is lukewarm much of the time, and we both talk in our sleep. As Louise De Salvo says in her book *Adultery*, affairs contaminate the air in a household as imperceptibly but as lethally as radon. Even the dictionary agrees. To "adulterate" means to despoil, dilute, poison, pollute, debase. It feeds feelings of helplessness, hopelessness, shame, and loneliness. There is no greater challenge to a love relationship.

And yet potential affairs are everywhere. Our work colleagues, our golf partner, the yoga instructor. We don't see them at their worst—when they are scared, sick, or just plain cranky. Lonely or dissatisfied with our existing relationship, we tell ourselves that it would be such a great break to just have a little fling, nothing big. An overnighter, maybe, or sex at lunchtime. "Nobody needs to know," we think. More than half of all married women have told themselves this.

And yet.

People find out. And people are hurt. Marriages break up or become bitter. We find that even if we shift partners, our lover-turned-spouse or -mate knows we have the ability to cheat. Maybe I've heard of a happy ending that grew out of adultery, but I can't remember it. On the other hand, I could fill a chapter of this book with the names of people who have had to piece their lives back together, who still have, broken hearts, because one of the partners strayed. We all deserve better.

What if you and I can't free ourselves from the pull of an affair? The forests of northern India are too far away, and Buddha is long gone. There are three pieces of advice the Buddha left us, three things that can give us the insight and energy not to be pulled astray: meditation, extreme mindfulness, and what I can only call "gross visual aids."

Meditation

First, it is useful to remember that all suffering comes from craving. This is the second noble truth. Over and over, Buddha taught his followers that moral discipline and meditation would protect them from straying. Moral discipline would come from seeing the harmful consequences of specific behaviors. Meditation was the channel that would allow for the viewing.

At its most basic level, meditation is a long, slow, sweet process of training our minds to relax—and then stay put. We breathe in and out slowly, in a quiet place. For a while—maybe even years—our minds are like puppies running here and there, bouncing all over the place. Yet once we are able to gently bring our minds back to our breathing whenever it races off, we find that, after a while, there is just the spacious, sweet breathing. Sometimes with less thinking. Sometimes with no thinking at all. Buddha instructed his followers to engage in meditation every day, urging them to put their whole being into the effort. If they did, insights would "be won," and a cool, calm, blissful, sorrow-free state would make itself known. He promised, "He who doth strenuously meditate, his shall it be to win the bliss supreme." [8]

Meditation can be done anytime and anyplace. Walking meditation can be as simple as walking back and forth across a small room or scurrying mindfully along huge city blocks. We can meditate quietly sitting on a couch or on a cushion. We can meditate when we can't sleep.

Meditation fosters appreciation for the things and people presently in our lives as we learn to accept and even enjoy our neurotic, monkey-minded selves.

Over the long haul, the practice of meditation will end the pull of an inappropriate affair because we can see more clearly what is really bothering us about our existing relationship. Usually it isn't the person, but the role.

When one of his female followers, wrestling with sensual cravings, asked Buddha what the point was when he told her to meditate, he responded that we naturally grow in five ways when we meditate, ways that will protect us from harming ourselves and the people around us. The five ways were in faith, in virtue, in learning, in generosity, and in wisdom:

> Who in this world in faith and virtue grows,
> In wisdom, generosity and love —
> A virtuous disciple, in this world
> She wins what is essential for herself. [9]

In a later conversation with his stepmother, Mahaprajapati, Buddha expounded on this teaching. When she asked for details about how to be virtuous, he gave her a list of things to avoid: greed, grasping, immodesty, unhappiness, sociability, sloth, and delight in doing harm. Meditating would show her where her tendencies toward each of these were, what situations would feed them. It would shield her against harmful actions.

Meditation as a protective shield against affairs?

Was he nuts?

For years I had a crush on a man who was extremely difficult (happily I wasn't in a relationship at the time; I can only imagine the damage that would have been done), a handsome, bad-boy type. An entrepreneur in a pickup truck, living with a woman he had told to move out but who had refused. Ignoring her behavior, he just started dating . . . me. He knew when to buy me roses and when to show up in the middle of the night.

I would go out with him for a couple of months, only to remember, each time, that we were a match that would never work. I'd have the courage to break off the affair and go through the throes of withdrawal. Then, each time, just when I was sure I was over him, he'd show up and we'd be back at it. It was an exquisite, romantic, heartbreaking dance. I went to therapy. Did all the things the therapist told me to do. Notes to myself on the refrigerator. A rubber band on my wrist to snap whenever I thought about him, especially the sex part. I had welts for weeks at a time. My best friends had vowed to keep me busy, and my mother had offered to take me in.

Nothing worked.

After the third iteration of our together/not together dance, I happened to read Buddha's teaching about the power of meditation. Deciding that I had nothing to lose, I signed up for a five-day meditation retreat, which proved to be a powerful jump-start to serious practice. (I had dabbled up to that point but had never quite decided to take meditation seriously.) At the end of the retreat, spurred on by the calm I had occasionally felt, I kept sitting in meditation at least once a day, and sometimes twice. When I started to think about him, I sat. And when I could feel that sinking yearning to be held (you know the one), I sat. I was a Zena Warrior Princess meditator, watching thoughts coming and going, sometimes sticking. For months I sat. Then, one night, I saw him walking up to my house, and I was able to say "no thank you." It wasn't easy, because to this day I wish we were a match, but we aren't and I knew it. Meditation had given me the space and distance I needed to be sane in my reaction to him. Crazy, huh? That was fifteen years ago, yet my heart still leaps into my throat when I see him. But that is all that happens. I can wait out the pull of the affair, which, these days, is only minutes long. Thank Buddha.

Mindfulness

Since meditation takes a while to kick in for most of us, we need a short-term assist. Two practices help; the first is mindfulness. This practice is about focusing completely on what we are doing. It is how we become aware of things as they really are. Stories abound in Buddhism about Zen masters who are considered to be extraordinary because "when they eat, they eat and when they sleep, they sleep." In other words, whatever they are doing takes all of their senses—seeing, hearing, tasting, touching, even thinking. There is no mental space available for fantasy, for affairs. When we are completely mindful there is simply no room for the pull of an affair because we are too caught up in exactly what we're doing.

With mindfulness we pay attention to the seemingly small things in our lives, such as how we pour a cup of coffee, where we set it down, and how we make our bed. Mindfulness takes us into a dimension where our bodies and our minds are in sync. So we aren't just pouring a cup of tea but noticing how lovely the cup is and whether the level of the tea is so high that it is only a question of where it will spill. With mindfulness we taste the different herbs in the tea, how they play together—a little sweet, a little spicy. We can feel the warmth of the tea fill our whole body.

Mindfulness literally demonstrates where there is work to be done—where we are careless, flip, and unthinking—as well as where and how we are nourished. We notice how good it feels to pick up the teacup in both hands, how happy we are when we have an entire hour of quiet all to ourselves. This information is useful. It gives us powerful clues regarding the areas in our lives where we need to smooth out the irritations and where we need to better support what makes us genuinely happy. To this day I remain convinced that mindfulness is a direct path to happiness regardless of what is going on in our lives. There is something wonderful about being fully present. It opens our hearts in a different way, into loving kindness for ourselves and for other people.

Gross Visual Aids

The second practice for short-term pulls? The women in Buddha's time trained themselves to do two things. The first was to meditate on the not-so-pleasant aspects of the human body: moles, wrinkles, cellulite, running noses, butt cracks— disgusting but effective when you spend time on it. If that didn't work, they zeroed in on the inside of the body. Picturing all the organs—the skeleton, blood, and other body fluids— reminded them that what they were attracted to was only a collection of body parts. The second thing they did, if mindfulness on the body failed, was remind themselves that the beauty of youth is all too quickly followed by old age and death. And they visualized watching their potential lover as a corpse being eaten by crows. That usually did the trick.

Living near the nuns was a young monk who was lucky enough to receive alms from Sirima, a young courtesan who, after trying to kill one of Buddha's followers, had vowed to feed eight monks a day to atone for her actions. When he went back to where the monks were staying, he couldn't say enough about Sirima. Her food was so good that he went into raptures. Only the best was offered, and so much of it that his portions alone could have fed three to four other monks as well.

But that wasn't all. Sirima was not only graceful and charming, she was also a knockout. One of the other monks, hearing him, fell in love with Sirima, sight unseen. The next day, he contrived to become one of the monks to visit her home. As karma would have it, Sirima was really sick that day. So when he showed up she was too weak to serve the monks. After they had eaten, she did manage to stumble into the room where they were sitting. Shaking from weakness, she paid her respects.

The young monk, already head over heels in love with his vision of her, was beside himself. "She looks radiantly beautiful even when she is ill! Imagine how great her beauty must be when she is well and wearing all her jewelry!" [10]

He was so in love he couldn't even function. Couldn't eat. Couldn't sleep.

Unfortunately, Sirima died that night. When Buddha heard the news, he decided to help the monk to let go of his obsession. Instead of cremating Sirima's body, it was placed in the charnel ground. While guards kept watch to make sure crows and other animals didn't eat her, the body decomposed in front of everyone's eyes, including the young monk's.

By day three the body was swollen.

By day four it was crawling with worms.

The young monk, seeing this, realized that his entire emotional reaction to her had been based on pure illusion. After a week or so, the Buddha gathered all of his followers together to warn them again about falling in love with a fantasy:

> "Here, monks, you see a woman who was loved by the world. In this same city, in the past, men would gladly pay a thousand gold coins to enjoy her for just one

night. Now, however, no one will have her, even for nothing. This is what the body comes to, perishable and fragile, made attractive only through ornaments, a heap of wounds with nine openings, held together by three hundred bones, a continuing burden. Only fools attach fancies and illusions to such an evanescent thing." [11]

The monk was cured.

It is a disgusting but powerful antidote, this corpse-watching trick. Just thinking about this story cures any fantasies I've had . . . once I'm willing to give them up.

Everybody Poops

When my son, Sarth, was two years old, his favorite book in the whole world was *Everybody Poops*. Each night he would ask me to read it to him again and again, until finally he knew it by heart and could say all the words with me. Even then he wanted me to read it to him. Whenever we finished he would fall asleep immediately. I tried not to think about what his dreams were like.

Other than at bedtime, the book never came up. Until one morning when we were on the six-thirty commuter bus headed for Portland. Suddenly, out of the early-morning quiet, a question: "Mommy, does he poop?" Sarth was pointing at the man sitting across the aisle from us. "Yes," I whispered. "Does she?" This time the finger was pointed at the woman kitty-corner to us, who always wore the same dress, a blue flower-print one.

"Yes."

He asked about three more people. My whispering didn't make him stop. Or any quieter. This was an important topic.

I noticed some smiles surfacing around us as he worked his way to the front of the bus. Sarth looked at the bus driver for a long time—through two bus stops.

"Does the bus driver poop?"

"I think so."

I heard a chuckle behind us.

"Mommy, do you poop?"

"I do."

By then the laughing out loud had started, and once we all gave into it the whole bus lit up—including the bus driver once he learned what was causing all the commotion.

Everybody poops.

At the time, a married man had a crush on me. I could tell because he kept showing up at my workplace just as I was going to lunch. Twice I caught him leaning on a lamppost outside of the city hall office where I worked. Then he asked me to have lunch with him. Three times in one month. Then twice in one week. He was fun and funny and cute. I was single parenting through a long, hard winter. Thinking about him one night, I was sitting on Sarth's bed reading *Everybody Poops*. Suddenly I had a vision of the man sitting on the toilet. Laughing out loud at the image, and myself, I realized in that moment how much I had let myself get caught up in fantasy. He was just a regular person with a family at home and a wife who loved him. I had no business spending time with him. So I stopped.

Everybody poops. Everybody has a downside, even our most acute fantasy partners, people we say we would walk to the end of the earth for. Everybody gets sick, throws up, smells bad sometimes, farts in bed. Everyone gets mad, and sad. Everyone fails sometimes and makes stupid mistakes. Everybody poops.

We're human. We aren't gods. This is a good thing to remember the next time you find yourself starting to put someone on a pedestal.

FREEDOM FROM THE PULL OF AN AFFAIR

Every once in a while Buddha would go for the jugular when he was concerned about someone getting distracted from their spiritual work. Then, as now, the pull of an affair kept popping up everywhere. If thinking of the person they were attracted to as their mother, sibling, or child didn't work, Buddha would describe the hells where people would land if they acted on the desire. The hell for having an affair with someone else's partner was the worst—limbs ripped apart while you drown in boiling oil. A helpful visual aid if internal organs and decaying bodies just isn't working for you.

Just so you know, Buddha knew the strength of this tug from his own experience. Even as a young man he was sensitive to the draw of sexual love. In a famous talk on desire he tells his followers that there is nothing in the world that binds the spirit of a man as much as a woman. When Buddha left home at the age of twenty-nine to take on the job of discovering the key to happiness through his spiritual efforts, he was starting on a path that would put him through all kinds of tests. For years he wandered as an ascetic, living by begging alms. For a while he even lived on three grains of rice a day. He didn't wash until he was so covered in grit and filth that insects called him home. He even withstood kids tickling the inside of his ears while he tried to meditate.

Finally, after six years of effort, some part of him knew that it was time to simply sit. He had already had the experience of deep samadhi, but recognized that there was still work to do. When he vows to sit under a Bodhi tree until he attains supreme wisdom, the pull begins. Mara, the lord of death and desire, decides that the time is ripe to go after Buddha full force. To knock him off his path. His weapon? He chooses the pull of an affair. If he can seduce the young Brahmin into an affair with one of his three indescribably beautiful daughters, then Siddhartha will never know the key to pure happiness. The daughters—appropriately named Craving, Discontent, and Lust—appear, dancing.

By this point Siddhartha has managed to move through all other desires. The only one left is the pull of an affair. He digs in. Meditates with everything he has, perfectly mindful. He is able to stay in mindfulness and to keep his concentration pure. In his effort he finds perfect freedom.

What is so powerful about this story is that it summarizes the antidote to affairs, that we need to concentrate on something other than the person who is tempting us. Maybe it's our work. Maybe it's our kids. Maybe it's our spiritual practice. Maybe it's our mate if we have one, or, if need be, a corpse. All of our senses need to be harnessed—and our energy. Siddhartha was burning a marathon worth of calories in this story. Vimala did the same thing later, as did all of the Buddha's women followers. Their reward? Freedom from the pull of affairs. And freedom from the other hindrances that had blocked their own waking up.

We might have to do the same thing. Energetic effort will sustain our mindfulness and concentration and push us over the wall of desire to freedom from the affair.

And when we are free the world rejoices, because we now represent one more moment where people won't be hurt—not our mate, our children, our extended families, our friends . . . or theirs. Best of all, we won't hurt ourselves.

.

Chapter Six
COMPETITION FOR OUR MATE

"The biggest betrayal has been women betraying women. Once the wound between women is healed, the wound between men and women can heal; once the wound between men and women heals, the family can heal; once the family heals, the community can heal; and once the community heals, the world can be healed."

— CHINA GALLANT, *The Bond Between Women*

WE ALL WANT what someone else has. And they want what we have if we happen to be married or mated to a halfway decent person. Women want other women's husbands. Men want other men's wives. The Buddha taught that dissatisfaction is part of the human condition. When it comes to mating he wasn't kidding. I remember living across the street from the perfect couple in the 1980s. The neighborhood was a Victorian village. Ten years younger than we were, they were drop-dead beautiful, both of them. He was an engineer who had just finished law school and was ready to take on the world. They had two adorable kids and grandparents who adored the whole lot.

One morning the young wife came over for tea. Walking in the door, she blurted, "I keep telling him I wish he was more like your husband! He never works on the house. Never brings me flowers." I admit it. For a split second I understood the draw of wife swapping. Before I gave in to the fantasy, I grinned and told her she was lucky to have a husband who loved her as much as he obviously did. The grass always looks greener from a distance.

THE CONSEQUENCES OF COMPETITION

One day King Pasenadi, leaving the city, looked up to see a beautiful young woman standing at the window of her house, looking down into the street.

In an instant he fell in love.

It turned into obsession before he even made it to the city gates. Determined to find out who she was, the king sent a flurry of attendants to scour the city for clues. Eventually, they learned her identity—a married woman.

No matter.

To be near her, the king hired her husband. Then he sent him on a special mission: to go to the underworld to collect lotus flowers and a special red clay for the king's bath. The young man was given a day in which to do it. If he wasn't back to the city by nightfall the king would have his wife.

Having no choice, the man sped out of the city at the crack of dawn the next morning. Just outside of the gate, planning his trip, he paused and shared his food with a stranger who obviously hadn't eaten in days. Throwing some rice into a nearby river he shouted into the air, "Oh guardian spirits! I have been generous sharing my food! Please be generous as well! I need a lotus flower and red clay for the king."

Done!

Since that hadn't been his first good deed, the earth immediately opened up. He was a pretty good guy: had shared his allowance as a kid, let schoolmates cheat off his palm leaves—that sort of thing. Meanwhile, the king, having a feeling that the young man might actually accomplish his task, had the city gates locked early. When the young man got to the first gate it was already locked. He stuck some of the red clay onto the walls, and flowers into the ground, and left, knowing in his gut that the king planned to kill him.

Back at the palace, the king was so obsessed with the young man's wife that he couldn't sleep. He lay awake thinking about how he had to make sure that the young husband was killed so he could have her.

Unfortunately, as is true in many Buddhist tales, things got a little wild for the king right about then. Moans and groans started coming out of the walls. Terrified, the king fled to see the Buddha, who explained that the sounds came from four dead men who had committed adultery in their lifetimes. They were now in hell.

Terrified, the king vowed on the spot never to covet another man's wife again. And he never did.

Staying Clear of Competition

The lesson of Pasenadi is this: We need to learn how to cherish what we have. When we put our energy into existing relationships rather than keep an eye out for a better deal, a funny thing happens. We fall in love with our mate over and over again. This does not mean that it's always easy to be in a relationship; there is always some level of difficulty. But we are better able to protect what we have when we keep our energy focused at home.

One way to accomplish this is to do gratitude practice every night. At the end of the day we take a couple of minutes to mentally list the things we appreciate about our mate and ourselves. We may be grateful that he comes home every day in time for dinner or that she remembers our birthday. He took the baby to the doctor. She did the week's laundry early so there would be enough clean underwear for the business trip. Gratitude practice protects us from being so drawn to outsiders that we neglect to notice what we have right in front of us.

If we still need an additional incentive it doesn't hurt to remember Pasenadi's four groaning ghosts. Rumor has it that adultery hell is one of the worst ones in the Buddhist pantheon. Burning oil, missing limbs, the constant smell of sulfur, you name it. It's a straight shot, I'm told. In case you needed a visual aid.

How Competition Affects the People around Us

> I asked Vivien if she thought Mrs. Walson was after her husband from the very start. 'Yes, I think she was.'
> — WILLIAM CASH, *The Third Woman*

When I was twelve, Graham Greene was my favorite author in the whole world. Though I had decided that my future wasn't going to be that of a Catholic nun after all, I was still fascinated by the Catholic Church. He made it human with his characters, with his Power and Glory priest, and with his themes of courage, tragedy, war, and guilt. I would read his books out loud, slowly, wondering what this man Graham Greene was really like, wondering where I would find him when I was old enough to marry.

Then I learned about his affairs—not just one, several,

maybe many. He was craziest in love with the American beauty Catherine Walston for years. They met in 1946 and were both married at the time. The weekend before that Christmas, Catherine decided to plunk herself down beside Graham at a dinner party and proceeded to steal his heart right in front of his wife, Vivien, his partner of almost twenty years. Did I mention that Vivien was also the mother of his two children and adored him? It didn't matter that Catherine had a reputation for having affairs, for seducing men and leaving them.

By the end of the meal he was a goner: "Greene was suddenly reminded again what happiness felt like. Catherine was intensely direct and frank with men, especially those she wanted to sleep with." [1] The two carried on for fifteen years:

> "I've dreamed of you all night dear heart. Vague, sad dreams. The cabin began being very big and homeless the first time I went into it, and I wish the type-writer wasn't there—it looks like a returned ring must look like on a desk. . . . An odd thing happened after you left: I fell in love with you all over again. Like when you dropped me at Oxford out of the airplane. It feels fresh and exciting and sad like then." [2]

They end up breaking each other's heart and the hearts of their spouses. Over and over, Graham threatened to leave his wife, never quite pulling it off. Sometimes it was because he knew Catherine was also carrying on an affair with the American general Lowell Weicker, and she might not give it up. Sometimes he didn't leave because Vivien threw herself at his feet, begging him to stay. They broke their children's hearts. And mine. Where was Greene's honor?

Falling in love with an inappropriate person harms many more people than we think. If we have children, they are harmed; not only have we betrayed them, we have also taught them at the deepest level that their own parent can't be trusted. Even if we are in a flat-out-forget-it lousy relationship, it is more upright to end that first. Children of adulterers have scars that may never heal in this lifetime.

Our parents are also harmed. They have a child who can't be loyal, who isn't able to protect her own home and family. There is so much shame in this for some parents that they are not able to continue a relationship with their own children. When this happens, our kids not only lose us, they lose their grandparents as well.

Our friends also suffer. If we can betray a mate, we can betray them. If we are capable of straying, how do they know their own mates are safe? Colleagues can experience the same fears. They get an added problem: Since adultery is consuming, our work typically suffers as well, which adds the additional burden of covering for us, cleaning up after us, and wishing that we were spending our workdays in another organization. If we lose too much time to the affair, our bosses will find a way to fire us. We risk everything in adultery. Not only the loss of our families, but of our friends, our homes, and our livelihood. No sex is that great.

SEEING SITUATIONS CLEARLY

It wasn't easy for mates during Buddha's time. It isn't easy now. Other people compete for our mates. What can we do? Buddha's teaching is always to first be clear about what is going on. If we think that our mate is having an affair, we need to verify that it is true as quickly and completely as we can. No disease can be cured until it is named. Someone moving in on our partner is a disease in our relationship.

Just be sure. As someone who has been falsely accused of wanting to have an affair, or of having an affair with someone else's husband, let me say that sometimes imaginations can be a lot more damaging than reality.

Fact vs. Illusion

For years, I taught a marketing seminar for high-growth companies in Michigan—Marketing 101. It was for owners who had managed to start successful companies but wanted to grow them faster and didn't know how. I usually taught it quarterly, mostly around metropolitan Detroit, in high-end hotels. At the end of a day at the Novi Hilton Hotel, a woman came rushing into the seminar room demanding to "speak with me." She was shaking so hard that she could barely get the words out of her mouth. I had no idea who she was and asked her if she could wait until the workshop participants left the room before we talked. She nodded yes. Then, as the last person walked out the door, she pulled a newspaper clipping out of her pocket. It had a picture of me on it, along with an announcement of the workshop.

"I know you're having an affair with my husband!"

She was shouting.

"I found this in his wallet!"

When I tried to tell her that I had no idea who her husband was she started yelling again.

"How could you?!"

The only reason I wasn't angry back was that she was so obviously heartbroken. After a couple of minutes she stopped yelling and stood there with tears in her eyes.

I asked her if we could call her husband together. Fortunately he was in his office. She got him on the phone and demanded to know what our relationship was. Told him I was standing there right next to her.

Silence for a couple of seconds. Then she handed the phone to me. Her husband told me that he had clipped the announcement out of the paper a year earlier because he wanted to take the class—stuck it in his wallet and then forgot about it. He apologized for what had happened. My response was that he was lucky to have a wife who really loved him. Maybe they could both come to a seminar together—my treat. He thanked me.

By the time I hung up the phone the woman was gone. I've not seen her since; I've never met her spouse.

In this land of competition for our mate we need to lean hard on Right Understanding. In other words, when we have that sinking feeling that something is amiss, it is important to separate fact from illusion. It is so easy to be carried away by our own imaginations. One false move on the part of our mates and we have climbed a ladder of inference so high that we're ready to take him to the cleaners. Before we do that, knowing how wrenching it is to pull a relationship apart, we need to see where we've made unfounded assumptions. We need to separate fact from illusion.

The place to start is simply to ask our partner. One phone call put an end to all that woman's fears about me. To this day, I don't understand why she just didn't ask her husband about the picture.

We know when our mates are lying. We sleep with them for heaven's sake. This is one time when I think it's okay to ask our partner just as he is waking up, "What's going on?" Ask before any defenses are in place. And if he or she gets angry, we can report the fear that grew out of our love and our gratitude for our life together. That we're sorry if we built a fantasy in our minds. Behind the initial irritation, most people will appreciate our caring about them enough to ask. And we'll be able to go back to living our lives without a cloud over our heads, one that was probably making us more than slightly difficult to live with.

Unfortunately, when someone is really competing for our mate, they are often all too eager to confess. In this scenario, all we have to do is ask her/him/them. "Are you after my husband/spouse/partner?" Floodgates open. Painful, visual gates. Hearing what someone has to say helps us to assess the damage done, if any. Then and only then can we deal with the reality of the situation.

State the Facts

Barbara has been married for twenty years to a man she adores. If you asked her to rank their marriage on a scale of one to a hundred, she would put it at ninety-five. They have the same interests, the same values, the same sense of humor. About a year and a half ago a younger woman showed up in their lives. A work colleague of her husband, Ben.

Troubled with her own marriage, the colleague began to ask Ben's advice. Before long they had graduated to daily conversations. Her husband even called Ben for advice regarding an affair he was certain his wife was having with another man.

Meanwhile, the woman and Ben were spending more and more time together, including planning a trip to a conference at a beautiful coastal resort on the East Coast. Barbara is beside herself with hurt, anger, and frustration. What can she do?

The women who followed Buddha had a strict tradition of

stating the facts of a situation before they responded to it. At least once a week, any interpersonal tensions were addressed. Sometimes it meant that one of the women ended up apologizing to another—or to the entire group—for her behavior. Sometimes it meant that amends had to be made—cleaning done, begging bowl rounds doubled.

Their lesson? Silent hurts fester. Our job, our spiritual work, includes surfacing everything we can so we can understand what is making a painful situation painful. When we understand what is really going on, we can address the problem. Our first task, when we discover that someone is deciding to share our mate, is to be clear about our reaction with our partner and, if we can, with the other person, too. This simple act often resolves the problem.

Barbara needed to find out how Ben and the other woman really felt about each other. How to find out? Ask. The only downside is that she could be wrong about the depth of their relationship. So what? Her concern only shows how much she loves Ben. To this day, I can still picture the woman at the Novi Hilton and see in her face her utter relief when she discovered I was safe. And hear the love she had for her husband in her voice, even as she cried.

Assess the Damage

Jocelyn, one of my dharma sisters, had been married for eighteen years when she discovered that her husband was having an affair. They had been each other's first real love; she married him right out of high school. They were my favorite couple for years—he was funnier than anyone I've met before or since, and she had a way of giving him plenty of space. He fed her creativity and she nurtured him.

Then he got a job in a city about two hours of driving away. They saw each other on weekends. Having been married for years by that time, the separation seemed to feed the marriage, reminding them of how much they loved each other. One weekend she decided to visit him in his new city. She called ahead, and he proposed that they meet at a small restaurant he had discovered—a small intimate place with fresh catch and good wine. As they were eating she noticed a woman staring at them. She asked her husband if he knew her.

"No."

Then the woman started sobbing uncontrollably. As Jocelyn got up to see if she could help, the woman walked straight over to their table.

"You can't keep us apart! We love each other."

Huh?

It turned out that her husband was having an affair. Had been for weeks. Furious, Jocelyn walked out and drove straight home. After a week of unprintable revenge fantasies, she was calm enough to call her husband to set up a meeting. While her ranting at him was a predictable response, her decision to visit the woman was not.

Instead of ranting, she just talked. She told the woman the story of their marriage, how they had met, what they meant to each other. She showed her pictures of their three daughters. She asked the woman to tell her what was going on. What were the facts of the situation? What advice would the woman give Jocelyn, knowing that she wanted to save her marriage? The woman looked at her, and started crying. After awhile she promised to move on. And she did.

Sometimes the last thing you want to do is to go into the dragon's mouth. Unfortunately, those early Buddhist women taught that that is exactly what we need to do in these difficult situations.

When someone has decided to go after our mate, if we are on a spiritual path, we are obligated to warn them of the damage being done by their behavior, even as we assess the damage that has already been done. This is only one woman's opinion, I admit. I've seen too many children suffer, too many friendships lost, too many careers hurt. We need to clarify these possibilities to the person intent on taking our mate if we can. If we can't say the words in person, then a letter or e-mail might be possible. Anything that can help him or her to see all the people who will be harmed by her actions is an act of kindness, I say. There is no such thing as a harmless affair. They all harm someone. They all break more than one heart.

By warning the other person about the damage he or she is causing, we are doing everything we can to help them stop. In its own way, this simple act can keep our own hearts open and the possibility of healing alive. If we can show compassion toward someone who is threatening life as we know it, then we'll also have compassion for ourselves when we need it. We aren't shutting down emotionally. We aren't running away from our problems. We are doing what we can to protect a genuine relationship. The ancient women would bow in our honor.

YOU AREN'T ALONE

Every woman I know has had to deal with someone competing for her partner. Apparently their looks don't cause it, because some of these mates are not physically attractive. Intelligence doesn't cause it either. And if her partner is powerful or wealthy, a whole slew of people might be standing in line.

Somehow, knowing that most women have had to face this issue helps us not to feel singled out. Helps us to stay sane while we figure out what needs doing, if anything.

In Buddha's time, a young woman named Kisagotami was married to a banker's son who treated her like garbage. Her in-laws were just as cruel. The only person who loved her was her little boy; then he died.

Kisagotami went nuts—literally. She dressed the dead toddler and carried him on her hip, going door to door, asking people for medicine. An old man told her that the only person he knew who had the right medicine was Buddha.

Kisagotami hunts him down and asks if he can cure her baby. He says yes but first she needs to get him a mustard seed from a house where nobody has died. She agrees. Going from house to house, the young mother discovers that everyone has known death—in one house it was in the past week, in another a year ago. In a third house a father died, in another a mother or a child. Not a single house was without death.

Suddenly realizing that everyone was in the same boat, Kisagotami is healed:

> The guide of a restless
> passionate humanity has said—
> to be a woman is to suffer.
>
> We have to understand suffering,
> the cause of suffering,
> its end . . .[3]

In the same way, knowing that we are not alone in this crazy, competitive world often helps.

And if our husband or mate has succumbed to the competition? Given that our biggest fear has just happened, our emotions can go haywire. Friends and family usually go haywire alongside us. We want revenge. When Louise DeSalvo told her friends that her husband was having an affair they told her to "kick the bastard out," that if they were in her shoes they'd pack up his clothes and give them to Goodwill, change the locks on the doors, and call a lawyer. One friend told her to hunt the lovers down and run them over. Another told her she couldn't stay friends with her unless she did something about the affair. Yet another said she would start returning Louise's calls after she demonstrated that she knew the meaning of revenge.

Instead of revenge, the Buddha taught us to see the situation clearly. And the way to do that is to get the facts. Friends who want us to seek revenge are simply demonstrating their own heartbreak on our behalf. Or, given the statistics on adultery, reliving their own trauma. It is okay to move down a different path of reactions—for your own sake—but getting the facts first gives us something constructive to do. Breaking the secrecy code also does two things: It tells us how serious the problem is, and it puts a spotlight on the real issues of the relationship.

People will tell us that our partner's adultery is not our fault. So what?! It still hurts like hell. It is hell. Knowing this, we learn that the only way out is through.

We assess the damage. Then we face the hardest questions. Assuming our partner wants to continue our relationship, will we stay or will we go? Whatever we decide—brace yourself—the only way through is to forgive the bastard or bitch and his or her coconspirator. Even when we would rather run them both over, having loved our best friend's suggestions, the only path out of hell is labeled "forgive."

In Buddhism, forgiveness is not about forgetting, it is about moving past something that has harmed us. Since "just forget about it" never happens in the case of adultery (I'm happy to be wrong here if you know of a case), we may as well take a deep breath and start the process. Otherwise we'll be enslaved by the betrayal for too long a time.

Forgiveness Matters

A few months ago I received a phone call from a good friend telling me that Molly's husband had fallen off their roof. He was in a coma and probably wouldn't live. I dusted of my *Tibetan Book of the Dead* and showed up at the hospital prepared for the worst. If you've never seen anyone in a coma with a roomful of machines forcing oxygen into the body, let me tell you, it's a scary sight. Instead of dying, his body insisted on staying alive. So I offered to be one of his sitters, to spend time with him chanting, reading quietly, or talking softly for as long as I could be helpful. Unsure of a reading topic, I wavered between erotica (figuring that at a minimum the doctors and nurses would spend more time in the room) and a book about forgiveness. The forgiveness book won.

The day after I read it to him he actually started talking and lifting his arms—not that I'm taking any credit, of course.

Sitting with someone who might decide to die at any minute has a way of forcing concentration. And thinking about what matters. As I looked at the man's lined face and watched him struggling to breathe, I suddenly realized that we all have lots to forgive. There's not a person among us who hasn't been deeply hurt at least once by someone else's action. And there isn't a person among us who is happy as a result of holding on to anger and hatred. So we need to forgive.

Forgiveness matters because it keeps our hearts soft. We can feel the compassion, gentleness, tenderness, and caring that is always there no matter how mucked up our lives may feel at the moment. Forgiveness is the path to peace because it gives us options. We can stay or we can go. We can love again, or still. In this way we keep an emotional door open so we can still be loved, and we all want that. Forgiveness frees us from our need, and hope, to change the past. It's over. Time to move on.

As bell hooks said in *All About Love*, "Forgiveness is an act of generosity. It requires that we place releasing someone else from the prison of their guilt or anguish over our feelings of outrage or anger. By forgiving we clear a path on the way to love. It is a gesture of respect." [4]

When we don't forgive, the physical symptoms alone can make us crazy. Here are just some of the ailments that can take over our bodies: headaches, backaches, pains in the neck, stomachaches, depression, a loss of energy, anxiety, irritability, tension, an "on edge" feeling, insomnia, and free-floating fear. Our whole immune system can even just shut down. According to intuitive healer, Caroline Myss, healing requires forgiveness. Why? Because forgiveness frees up the energy we need to heal ourselves.

And finally, in case it still matters, forgiveness is the best revenge, because the person or people who caused us pain no longer have a lock on our brain.

FOUR STEPS THROUGH ANGUISH

Deciding that you are willing to at least try, there are four huge steps that can move us through the anguish of adultery—

actual or intended. We can be gentle with ourselves. This is a pain that makes us feel fragile. We need to take care of ourselves. At the same time we need to let ourselves be angry if that is our reaction. Anger happens. It is a natural response to a threat. And we've been plenty threatened. At the same time, it is hugely helpful to do our best to change the lens we've been using to look at the world—to trade ours in for that of the person who has zeroed in on our mate. This shift can create an empathy that will make it easier for us to know what to do next. Finally, we need to take a deep breath and just "pull the arrow out" of our hearts. So we can heal cleanly.

Be Gentle with Yourself

First, we need to be completely gentle with ourselves. The core precept in Buddhism is "Do no harm." It is easy to forget that you and I are included here. So instead of eating a freezer's worth of frozen chocolate bars, swallowing sleeping pills, having sex with an inappropriate partner, consuming large quantities of alcohol, or driving our car in a way that is dangerous to ourselves and others, we need to treat ourselves as completely precious beings. For me that means healthy food, a little chocolate—the best kind of course—clean cotton sheets, and a new book to read, one with a happy ending. Being gentle with myself means not calling a relative who, within minutes of the beginning of our conversation, will remind me of the ways I've failed him over the years. When I'm tired, being gentle with myself might mean not answering the telephone after 9:00 P.M. or going to bed early. Mostly, this step is about being our own best friend and filling our minds and space with as much loving kindness as we possibly can. Here is a meditation that always helps:

Close your eyes and begin to relax, exhaling to expel tension. Now center the normal flow of the breath, letting go of all extraneous thoughts as you passively watch the breathing in and breathing out. . . . (Let your consciousness move outside of your body to the earth and then beyond the earth.) Now, as if out there from interstellar distances, turn and behold our own planet, our home. . . . See it suspended there in the blackness of space, blue and white jewel planet turning in the light of its sun. . . . Slowly . . . approach it, drawing nearer, returning to this part of it, this region, this place. . . . And as you approach this place, let yourself see the being you know best of all . . . the person it has been given you to be in this lifetime. . . . You know this person better than anyone else does, know its pain and its hopes, know its need for love, how hard it tries. . . . Let the face of this being, your own face, appear before you. . . . Speak the name you are called in love. . . . And experience (a) strong energy current of loving-kindness, how deeply you desire that this being be free from fear, released from greed and hatred, liberated from ignorance and confusion and the causes of suffering. . . . The great loving-kindness linking you to all beings is now directed to your own self . . . now know the fullness of it. [5]

So be gentle with yourself first and always.

Anger Happens

Second, it is okay to be angry. In a perfect world, none of us would be, given the huge karmic costs of anger. But it's not a perfect world in the sense of there being no pain—pain and betrayal are the things that can outrage even the most gentle woman.

Anger is simply a strong form of energy, and a useful one if it can be channeled. An effective way to channel anger is to write a letter to the woman competing for your husband or lover and, if an affair has already started, a letter to your mate. There are specific ground rules for this writing:

- You need to be in a quiet, safe-for-you place—I use my dining room.
- You need to have at least one uninterrupted hour. The phone needs to be turned off and the blinds drawn if you have friends or neighbors who like to pop in.
- The letter has to be handwritten. That way your entire body is involved, and you can really think about what you want to say.
- You need at least ten pages of blank paper for each letter.

Then, with a cup of tea or coffee within reach, write on the top of the first page, "I am so furious," and just keep writing until your hand can't write anymore or you run out of things to say. Don't stop until you can feel your emotional energy shift. You'll cry. It's okay. You might even laugh. That's okay, too. Don't edit. Say everything. When you are completely spent, read the letter, out loud is good, and then burn it or rip it into shreds.

When I met the love of my life it took me all of three weeks to fall head over heels in love with him. I assumed he was single. After a passionate love affair I was stunned to learn that he was married but that his wife had been away for the summer. He told me about her the day before she was supposed to come home. Crushed and angry, I bought a dozen roses for him to give to her, said good-bye, and was heartbroken beyond words.

A few weeks after she got back he showed up at my door—they had separated. Weak with yearning, I was thrilled to see him. For about six months we had one of those romantic love affairs you read about in books—he even followed me out west. Then his wife started calling my apartment, every day. She wanted him back, would do anything. One day he was gone before I came home from work.

I wallowed in my misery for several weeks. Then I decided that enough was enough. I went home, took a bubble bath, and started writing the letter. By the end of it, some twenty-two pages later, all of them tear-stained, I found myself apologizing to his wife. She deserved to try to mend the marriage. They had been together since high school. If I had known he was married our affair wouldn't have happened. Although I shredded the pages, that letter was the door to forgiveness—of him, her, and me.

Seeing the World through Their Eyes

Step three? Walk a mile in her shoes. A surprising but effective method for letting go is to take some time to tell yourself, or write about, the competitor's story. Part of why Uttara was able to forgive Sirima was because she knew her story—that she didn't have a permanent home or partner. The biggest reason why I was able to forgive my partner's estranged wife was because I was able to feel what she must have felt. By then I also knew enough of their story to know the sacrifices she made for him, to see how her former casualness about his affairs got them both into trouble when I showed up. And knowing his story, his tragic childhood and how only brilliance and athleticism got him up and out of abject poverty, helped me to understand just about everything that happened in our three-person dance. I wasn't any less heartbroken, but I knew I would heal because I knew the facts. I had faced my own anger with gentleness and could see the situation through all three sets of eyes.

My friend Penny insisted on meeting her husband's lover face-to-face once she was certain they were having an affair. She was so nervous about it that her entire body was covered with hives the day of the meeting, a luncheon. No matter. Off she went to meet Barbara. The rest of us held our breath, waiting for news of the meal. When we all gathered at her house later that afternoon, she was incredulous. She had liked the woman. Felt sorry for her because she was trying to raise two young sons on her own, having been abandoned by her husband and her family (for crossing racial lines). Penny's husband had been the first person to show the woman any empathy. She was so grateful to him. They had started eating lunch together and, well, one thing led to another.

"I actually sat there trying to figure out how we could share the son of a bitch."

Let Go
Step four: Pull the arrow out. When people asked Buddha about difficult emotions and events, he taught that the way to get past anything is to simply let go:

> Suppose a man were pierced with a poisoned arrow. And
> his friends and relatives got together to call a surgeon to
> have the arrow pulled out and the wound treated. If the

wounded man objects, saying, "wait a little. Before you pull it out, I want to know who shot this arrow. Was it a man or a woman? Was it someone of noble birth or a peasant? What was the bow made of? Was it a big bow or a small bow? Was it made of wood or bamboo? And what was the bow string made of? Fiber, or gut? Before you extract the arrow, I want to know all about these things." Before all this information can be secured, no doubt the poison will have time to circulate all through the system and the man may die. The first duty is to remove the arrow, and to stop its poison from spreading.

In the search for truth there are certain questions that are unimportant. If a person were to postpone his searching and practice enlightenment until such questions are solved, he would die before he found the path. [6]

The same truth holds here. Once we know the facts, have vented our anger and heartbreak on paper, and have considered the competitor's situation, we need to let go. In the letting go our next step will be clear. Maybe we need to live on our own. Maybe we need to go away with our mate to negotiate a process for building a relationship. Maybe we just need a full vacation from each other for a while—say thirty days— before we come back together to decide what to do. Maybe we decide we can share.

COMPETITION IS ALWAYS going to be out there. Sometimes it will be mostly harmless—a little flirtation here and there. Sometimes it will rock our relationship at its very roots. Our job is to keep our heads unclogged, to see situations clearly. If our worst fear happens, if our mate does end up in someone else's arms permanently, there are things we can do rather than going after both of them with our best kitchen knife. We can separate fact from illusion. Find out what the real story is. And then we can forgive, so we can move on with our own life. You just never know. Forgiveness makes all sorts of things possible. It leaves doors open, makes children safer, and protects us from the negative karma that would have attached itself to our body-minds had we given into revenge. Amen.

Chapter Seven

SURVIVING THE LOSS OF A LOVER

There was once a great Tibetan teacher named A-Yu Khadro who lived to be 115 years old, and Norbu Rinpoche, a well-regarded Tibetan monk, studied with her. A-Yu Khadro was drawn to the dharma at the age of seven and she practiced, with her aunt, until she was nineteen. That year, her parents arranged for her to marry a kind, gentle man. A-Yu tried to be a good wife, but became deathly ill by the third year of their relationship. Terrified that she would die, her husband called a psychic for help. The psychic said that A-Yu would indeed die if she was not freed from the marriage so she could focus on her spiritual practice. Facing the loss of his beloved wife, her husband had to decide what to do. "My husband was a very kind man and agreed that if married life was endangering my life it must be stopped." He loved A-Yu so much that he promised to carry her to a cave where she could practice. He would be her patron, bringing her food and supplies.

Their marriage was dissolved. Within the first year of doing her spiritual practice she recovered.

The two remained close friends for the rest of their lives.

—PARAPHRASED FROM CHINA GALLANT,
The Bond Between Women

THERE IS A COMPANY in Atlanta, Georgia, that specializes in scorned-woman products. Its Scorned Woman Hot Sauce, packaged in a black velvet bag, is a "devilish temptation of Tabasco, habanero and onion." The Scorned Woman Fiery BBQ Sauce offers the same tempting blend, promising to revenge any heartbreaks caused by imperfect former boyfriends, lovers, partners, and husbands. If only the healing of heartbreaks were so easy.

As any magazine or Internet poll will attest, one of the most gut-wrenching experiences in any person's life is the surprise abandonment by a lover or spouse. When it happens, we reel, we blame, we rage. Our friends tell us to "conjure up a scenario that's savagely wicked or hilariously humiliating, and replay it satisfyingly often in your mind. Maybe his prized comic book collection goes up in the flames of a fire he carelessly starts. Or perhaps he finally meets his celebrity dream girl—and she proceeds to tell him she's heard what he did to you and thinks he's the scum of the earth." [1]

We plot to get even. In the heat of her rage, a woman I once worked for threatened to file random change-of-address forms so her former husband would no longer get his mail delivered. A male acquaintance parked his car outside his ex-lover's house, headlights aimed at her bedroom window, so he could keep her room lit all night, keeping her from sleeping. When Emilienne Bey, one of Cairo's Grande Dames of the early twentieth century, discovered that her husband had secretly impregnated a much younger beauty, she donated their mansion and Egypt's finest collection of European Impressionist paintings to the state to keep all of her husband's assets out of the hands of the young woman and any children she had.

Getting over abandonment by a lover can take years. A

friend of mine once told me that he finally stopped obsessing about a lover who had walked out on him five years after their relationship ended. And even then a mere mention of her name or a glimpse of her picture could kick-start a tailspin of negative emotions: Where is she now? Who is she with? How could she have left?

Popular magazines are bursting with advice for dealing with such a loss. "Stay busy," they tell us. Wear a rubber band around your wrist and snap it every time you start to think of him or her. Get rid of his stuff, they warn, if you want to move on with your life. Prescribe some personal painkillers: "Feel free to indulge the urges that dull the ache, no matter what your well-meaning friends advise . . . rent super-sappy videos, eat takeout in your pajamas, and confront your agony so it doesn't turn you into a bitter, bitter woman." [2]

It needn't be so.

LETTING HIM GO

One of the most beautiful tales from Buddha's time is the love story between a young woman named Capa and a young ascetic, Kala. Capa grew up happily in a well-to-do household. Her father, a trapper, deeply believed that one could gain spiritual merit by feeding the monks who would appear at the doorstep of the family compound on their early-morning alms rounds. The trapper was grateful that he could afford to be generous, and he instilled in his daughter a sense of obligation about caring for spiritual seekers.

Growing up, Capa was given many of the respo   f running a household. Apparently, she did so wel' father began going off on hunting excursions f time, knowing that his spunky teenage daugh' any demands that surfaced. One of her most important responsibilities, in his absence, was to provide food for the monks.

One morning Capa made an offering to a young mendicant named Kala. His experience of her generosity was one of love at first sight, a reaction that was quite rare in those days. So struck was he by her energy, her graceful movements, and her beauty that, at first, he could not move. Finally, staring at the woman, his heart in his eyes, he silently swore to himself that she would be his wife.

There was more: If he couldn't have her, he would starve himself to death.

Six days later, when Capa's father returned from hunting and asked his daughter about the young monk who used to come to the door for alms every day, she reported that he had only appeared one time. Her father, worried, went looking for Kala, finally finding him weak with hunger. The young man confessed that he was in love with the trapper's daughter and that he had made a vow to starve himself if they weren't married. The older man was so struck by Kala's fervor that he consented to the marriage.

A wedding was held. The couple was deliriously happy at first and even had a child together. But as is true for too many "love at first sight" relationships, they discovered that they didn't get along so well when tested by time. Even though they meditated together, their relationship just didn't gel. When Capa was unhappy, she would complain of the imperfections in their relationship. In turn, Kala would threaten to leave. Finally, one day he simply packed up, preparing to abandon her.

Seeing his set jaw, Capa was terrified of her pending loss. At first she tried to seduce him. So far her's is a familiar reaction.

If you haven't tried it yourself, you probably know someone who has. But then crazy wisdom kicked in. Realizing that Kala really was leaving, she simply stopped. She stopped the seduction, stopped arguing, and just let him go. Right then and there. With no regrets. No blame. No revenge. And vowed to remain his friend and spiritual sister for the rest of their natural lives.

Here is their story from the Therigatha, a collection of enlightenment poetry that is almost 2,500 years old:

> KALA:
>> Once I was an ascetic with a stick in hand.
>> Now I am a deer hunter.
>> It's because of my own lust
>> that I'm in this swamp
>> and can't see my way clear
>> to the other shore.
>> Capa thinks I love her;
>> she has kept our son happy.
>> But I want to cut my ties with her
>> and renounce the world again . . .

> CAPA:
>> Kala come back!
>> Enjoy my love.
>> I'll be your slave
>> and all my relatives too.

> KALA:
>> If even a part of what you say were true,
>> Capa,

that would be terrific for
someone who was turned on by you.

CAPA:
  Oh Kala,
  I am like a Takkara tree
  blossoming on a mountain top,
  like a bitter-apple vine in flower,
  like a trumpet flower in the interior of an island.
  My body has been rubbed
  with golden sandalwood paste.
  I have put on muslin from Varanasi.
  I am beautiful.
  Why do you leave me?

KALA:
  You are like a bird-hunter
  with that lovely body of yours,
  but you won't snare me. . . .

CAPA:
  Then good-bye, Kala.
  Where will you go?
  To a village, a town, a city, a capital?

KALA:
  . . . now by the Neranjara River
  the Buddha teaches the Dharma to the living.
  I'll go to him;
  he'll be my teacher.

CAPA:

Then give him my greetings,
the guide of the world,
and make an offering for me.

KALA:

It's right, what you say Capa.
I'll give him your greeting,
the guide of the world,
and make an offering for you. [3]

Accepting Reality

Here's the brilliance of Capa's reaction. In her simple acceptance of her reality she opens a way for them to hold on to a
much deeper relationship, one that is free from any anger or
resentment, one that later nurtures her as she practices meditation and attains her own enlightenment. It didn't matter that
he was from Mars and she was from Venus. What mattered
was the reality of their situation and her deep willingness to
encase it with all the compassion she had to offer. It took
courage. And it worked.

Capa went on to raise their son and to concentrate on her
own spiritual work. She became a follower of the Buddha and
his teachings and quite well known as a compassionate and
wise woman capable of offering her own teachings. Most of
all, she was able to deepen her practice to where she had her
own experience of enlightenment and with that the everlasting
peace for which we all yearn.

What are the gifts Capa offers to us? She teaches the truth
of the power of letting go. She didn't want to. With all her
heart she wanted Kala to stay with her. He was the love of her

life. Her mate, the father of her child. She was willing to do what she thought it took to keep him, to be his slave, to seduce him. But his yearning for spiritual work was too deep. Like all of us, Capa learned that our love for each other can only be one component of our lives, not all of it. Our mates need other interests, are often pulled by other yearnings, deeper ones than the love of a mate.

Capa demonstrates the skill of moving from struggling to a grace-filled acceptance of what is. In her shift she demonstrates a love beyond words, a willingness to take on a broken heart if that is what Kala needs from her. Hers is an unselfish act, an act of unconditional love. This is an immeasurable gift. For someone to love us so much that they are willing to step aside so we can follow our deepest passion is love worth waiting lifetimes for if that's what it takes. Capa's life is proof that we can all sort through the components of our relationships, saving the parts that can nurture and support our best selves and the best self of our beloved and throwing the rest of the lot into a hell-realm dumpster. What a role model.

Learning to Let Go

After thirteen years as best friends, Ann and John became lovers. They were joined at the hip for a while there, but a year into the relationship they had their own personalities back and were happily married. Their only problem was that John is an adventurer, and even though he loved Ann as much as I expect he would love any woman, adventure is adventure. I remember hearing the first hints that things weren't perfect in their private Nirvanaworld. He hadn't been on the road lately. His friend Mike was going to Europe to kayak for a month.

Ann started to cling, and seduce. Her clothes got sexier. She came home from work in time to cook dinner every night. I didn't realize people still did that.

John talked more and more about traveling. The books he brought home were about trailblazers and ecowarriors. Ann called me, terrified she was going to lose him. Did I have any ideas? At the time I didn't, because when my friends are terrified I'm quite skilled at getting equally scared. But then I remembered Capa and Kala and sent her their story. Nothing. About a month later, news. John had left for an adventure—no time limit. He'd get back when he got back. Ann even took him to the airport. I was stunned at how happy she sounded and had to ask what happened.

"I just let go," she told me. "I told John that I knew in my heart of hearts that he was going to leave eventually, no matter what I said or did. So I decided that I would just concentrate on being his best friend and help him pack."

Ann really loved John. She was terrified of losing him, terrified he'd find another woman, meet her on the plane. Yup, he'd get on the plane and this amazingly beautiful woman would just happen to be in the next seat and they would talk about kayaking—it would be her favorite sport, the sport that landed her in the last Olympics. He'd be in love by the time they landed. It made Ann nuts just thinking about all the possibilities.

Sick with fear, Ann decided that she just had to let go, since she had absolutely no control over John's behavior. Instead of just sitting in meditation, she decided to use a mantra, a phrase she could repeat over and over, to help her when she was most scared. She didn't have the energy to sit, she told me. Heartbreak can do that sometimes.

So Ann chose reciting her mantra of "Don't know" as her letting-go practice. With every out-breath she would just think the phrase "Don't know." Her "don't know" mind helped her to let go of the fears—at first the big, juicy, neurotic ones, finally the small persistent ones. She realized pretty quickly that her experience of John was that he loved her, wherever he was and whoever he was with. Her terror of losing him morphed into a contentedness about their relationship.

John heard it in her voice whenever he called—the lack of clinging, the simply caring about his well-being. He in turn felt free to love Ann in his own way, and wrote some of the best love letters I've ever had the pleasure of reading over someone's shoulder. Maybe their evolved relationship won't last. Or maybe it will. The main thing is that they have managed, through Ann's open-hearted crazy wisdom, to create a partnership that continues to be precious to both of them instead of positioning them as victim and victimizer.

If she hadn't let him go I'm pretty sure the two would not still be together. They would not have the friendship they share, the privilege of shared growth. In letting John go, Ann also gave herself permission to look at her own passions. She has always loved to write, and to draw. Over time, she's done more and more of both. If there is a happier woman I don't know her.

Letting Go to Save a Friendship
I guess it helps to have been married a couple of times when you're writing a book about relationships. I've had a firsthand look at how the different ways one ends a marriage and a love affair impacts the rest of your life. Wayne John Randall is one of my best friends in the whole world. He and I were married

until he got our marriage annulled in Australia about five years ago. I will love him until my last breath, and it will be just fine with me if he is my mother in our next go around on earth.

We met in Australia, where I spent a good part of my growing up. He was one of my stepbrother's best friends—the one who made sure everyone made it home to the correct bed after partying hard on the beach or at a neighborhood pub. In the group of young men who could each make the cut for a cover photo on *GQ*, Wayne John was the scruffy, shaggy, blond-haired one—half surfer, half truck driver. We had a blast traveling in a pack, the group of us. Long days at the beach pretending to surf, running, swimming. It was even fun to grocery shop together for our assorted families. Wayne John was always fun, always there for the rest of us.

Year's later, my marriage with my daughter's father was ending. Although we had been separated for six months, there was still a part of me that wanted to salvage the marriage. We had both worked on the relationship for so long. (Is this sounding familiar?) To get a grip on my life, I took a trip back to Australia. I wanted to spend time in the sun, remember how to surf, be with people who just plain cared about me—no strings attached.

I never expected to fall in love. Not with one of my best pals. I'd like to say that I stayed and spent the rest of my life in tropical bliss once the light of love dawned, but I didn't. After a couple of weeks of R and R, my job, family, and almost estranged husband were in Michigan. Without my saying much, Wayne John realized I had fallen in love with him. He didn't do anything about it, so I can't even report wild and wonderful tantric sex. We spent my last day in Australia together attending another friend's wedding and talking late into the night as best friends. The next morning he drove me to the airport and let me go.

I came home to four more years of doing my damnedest to make a mismatch-from-hell marriage work, not willing to admit failure. My husband worked just as hard from his end. Wayne John called me only once, to make sure I made it home okay. And I wrote him only one or two letters—too afraid of the emotions tucked between the words. "That was that," I told myself.

After I had been divorced for six years, the phone rang in the middle of the night on a New Year's Eve. It was Wayne John. "I've decided you're the one and I'm coming to get you." A hugely romantic moment if you're wide awake, which I wasn't. I figured it had been a wrong number, not recognizing the voice, and went back to sleep. Happily he called again and spent the next two years flying halfway around the world on a regular basis to spend time with me—even living in the temple as a non-Buddhist resident, since I was in the seminary at the time.

Gun-shy, I hesitated to react to his advances. I had made a vow to my daughter to stay in Ann Arbor until she was eighteen, ruling out any possibility of moving to Australia. Wayne John had a small successful business in Queensland, one that needed him every day.

But romance is romance.

One summer afternoon, about a year and a half into his visits, driving back from a camping trip to northern Michigan, Wayne John suddenly stopped on the side of Highway 131. "I'll back you whatever you want to do with your life. Please marry me."

I did.

We figured we would have a two-continent marriage until Jamie was eighteen. The first summer I went to Australia, where Wayne John built us a tree house for grown-ups to live in. He backed it up to a rain forest so we had miles of nature behind us. We talked about building me a tiny meditation cabin at the back of the property, complete with a stream and bamboo grove.

Three months later, back in the States, Wayne John called me from Queensland. A long-distance marriage didn't work for him. He was going to hire someone to take over his business so he could move to Ann Arbor. Which he did . . . in the dead of winter . . . with no friends here and two metal pins in his leg, which chilled his entire body whenever the temperature dropped below freezing. It was the coldest Michigan winter in a decade.

Within the first week, Wayne John started sleeping around the clock, not getting up for meals, just barely getting up for weekend excursions. To tell you the truth, I thought he was dying. It was like watching a beautiful flower suddenly start to shrivel. I was so scared I tried to ignore his behavior, but after about three days I finally had the courage to ask what was wrong.

"I'm so homesick I wish I was dead."

The minute he said the words I knew it was true. He had left lifelong relationships behind, a house of best friends, his income. Sunny spring days had been traded in for a harsh Michigan winter that can make just about anyone miserable, even lifelong Michiganders. He had traded joking around and casual conversations with strangers to people frowning at him every time he opened his mouth, not understanding his accent. He had traded a house with a wraparound porch and no locks for a tiny basement apartment with two layers of alarm systems.

He had to go home.

Jamie was only twelve.

I was facing pure abandonment—not only by my husband but my best friend. No words could come out of my mouth. Instead, I went outside and walked in circles around our apartment complex, feeling too whacked out to do anything else. Wayne John was leaving. I didn't even have anger to use for energy, since it wasn't like he was committing some relationship mortal sin.

Still, it was a body blow. I loved him; still do. He was my best friend, still comes close. I knew that Buddha had taught ad nauseum that dharma love is about friendship first. I finally decided to try to just be his friend, just like Capa and Ann—even though it was uncharted territory for me. Particularly in the face of pure abandonment.

I asked Wayne John how I could help him. "Put me on a plane." To tell you the truth, I didn't have the courage to go to the airport—it hurt way too much. But I was able to tell him that I wished him well. And learned to love him in a whole different way. When he told me last year that he had finally re-married, I was genuinely happy for him and thrilled for his wife. She's a lucky woman.

Looking back, it was choosing to defend our friendship that protected me and made it possible for me to love him still. Some of my best friends told me I was nuts. But it worked. I kept hearing Buddha's words like a CD that keeps skipping to the same spot: friendship is everything, friendship is everything, friendship is everything. . . . Friendship is everything: "This is the entire holy life, Ananda, that is, good friendship, good companionship, good comradeship. When a [person] has a good friend, a good companion, and a good comrade, it is expected that he will develop and cultivate the good." [4]

How did I let go? I knew from the stories of the ancients that the only way to protect what we still have is to cough up all expectations and spit them out. So I did. Every time anger surfaced, or hurt, or anguish, I just sat with it. Right in its belly. Sometimes I sat crying. Sometimes I sat while my body hurt so much that I was sure someone or something was actually burning my skin. I knew that if I gave in to any negative emotions we were screwed. The friendship would be lost.

So I sat in meditation every chance I got: in the morning, at lunch, when I came home to an empty apartment. I made myself sit when it was the last thing I wanted to do, just breathing in and out, sometimes whispering to myself "let go."

It took a couple of weeks to get a grip. Pretty short period of time, given all the emotions I was able to move through. By Wayne John's third week back in Australia I was glad when he called. I was glad he was still my friend.

And if friendship can't work? The new partner is jealous? Your lover or ex-husband wants nothing to do with you? You want nothing to do with him? Nothing to do with her? Or maybe he died? Let go. Just let go. Let go by gently reminding yourself—every time he or she pops up in your head—that the relationship you had is now past tense. Over and over, you can say the mantra to yourself as a loving best friend: "It is in the past. Let go. Let go. Let go." Crazy wisdom. If you are anything like me, at first just thinking the mantra may trigger overwhelming feelings of hurt, anger, rage, vengeance plots. When it does we can write, chant, walk, do prostrations, scrub floors, and then say the mantra again and again. When our heart aches we can do our spiritual practice, using the abandonment as energy for our own enlightenment. The greater the abandonment, the stronger the energy.

LOVE DOES NOT EQUAL HAPPINESS

Sometimes, no matter how hard we try, the marriage or love affair simply won't work. Isadasi was another follower of Buddha. She showed up asking to be a nun when she was still a young, beautiful teen. When an older nun, Bodhi, asked her what made someone "in the flush of her youth" decide to become an ascetic, Isadasi told her that her bad luck marriages had driven her to the Buddha.

Isadasi had been raised in the kingdom of Avanti by a wonderful family. When one of her father's business friends asked for Isadasi's hand for his son, her father was delighted and agreed to a marriage. As was the custom, after the wedding Isadasi went to live with her in-laws, where she tried very hard to be a good wife and family member. Rather than depend on servants, she cooked all of her husband's meals, washed all his dishes, and showed him "devotion unsurpassed."

Unfortunately, he hated her. He was furious with his father's choice and complained bitterly to his parents, who had no idea what he was talking about. They had found Isadasi to be a devoted spouse and daughter-in-law. When they asked him what she was doing wrong he said, "Nothing." He just didn't like her.

"He explained that she certainly had done nothing to hurt him, nor had she ever displayed any aggression against him, but he simply did not like her, he was tired of her, he had had enough of her, and he was ready to leave the house so that he would not have to set eyes on her anymore." [5]

Well.

His parents, not having a clue how to respond to him, asked Isadasi to come to talk to them. Promising not to harm her in any way, they told her what their son had said. Had he left anything out? Isadasi was shocked:

> I rose early and went to my lord's room,
> having already washed my hands and feet,
> and on the threshold I came up to him
> with cupped hands.
> Bringing comb, mirror, soap,
> and ornaments as though I were a servant,
> I dressed him and groomed him myself.
>
> I boiled the rice,
> I washed the pots,
> and looked after him
> as a mother would her only son.
>
> And though I was devoted to him,
> a humble and affectionate servant,
> who was virtuous
> and got up early,
> my husband felt nothing for me. [6]

She had done nothing offensive. It didn't matter. Even though their son's hating her was irrational, his parents were forced to send her away.

Returning home, the young woman faced a father determined to find her a suitable husband. Given her beauty, it wasn't long before a local businessman came forward to ask for her hand in marriage. Because he was older Isadasi's father was hopeful he would have more patience, be more gentle.

Nope.

Within a month Isadasi faced rejection. Even though she loved her new husband and served him with "utmost love and affection" it did not protect her from his abandoning her. Within weeks he became so irritated by her very presence that he sent her back to her father's house, demanding an annulment.

By this point, her entire family was at a loss about what to do next. Isadasi was determined to prove that she knew how to be a good wife. Her father was desperate to find her a home. The problem was that none of the eligible men were interested. Just as her parents were about to give up, an ascetic showed up at the door begging for alms. In a moment of inspiration, Isadasi's father asked if he would consider trading in his ragged clothing and begging bowl for a beautiful wife. To sweeten the deal he would also throw in a mansion.

The ascetic agreed, and a marriage ceremony was held.

But then . . .

This time, after only two weeks the mendicant fled to his father-in-law's house begging for his robe and bowl. He would rather starve to death than spend another day in Isadasi's company.

Her entire extended family pleaded with him to stay. They would fulfill his every wish. Anything he wanted.

He said no.

All he knew was that he could no longer stay under the same roof with her. Picking up his robes and grabbing his bowl, he fled.

To be rejected by three husbands in a row can be pretty

devastating. Beside herself, Isadasi decided to commit suicide. As she was planning the deed, a Buddhist nun walked by her parent's front door on an alms round. Seeing how peaceful she looked, it occurred to Isadasi that she needed to let go of her obsession with being married. Maybe this was simply not her time.

She begged her father to let her become a nun. At first he refused—she should stay with her family, safe under their roof. The young woman wept and wailed until he gave in.

Isadasi became a nun. Immediately following her ordination she spent seven days meditating, determined to scrape all the heartbreak out of her heart.

It is said that the young woman's practice was so strong that she saw her past lives. In one of them she saw why marital bliss didn't have a chance. Eight lifetimes ago she had been a man—a handsome and rich goldsmith. When she wasn't working she was seducing other men's wives, the first Don Juan. She had been addicted to seduction, breaking heart after heart, destroying marriage after marriage. And when she died as the goldsmith, her karma followed her. No wonder her marriages didn't work. It wasn't her fault, and it wasn't worth losing another night's sleep over. Isadasi let everything go, just like that.

Follow Your Heart

Isadasi realized that love relationships aren't what happiness is all about. They just aren't. Peace and contentment can never come from external factors, because anything external to our own heart is always changing. Even a perfect love relationship as defined by *Elle*, *Cosmopolitan*, or even Oprah could be gone tomorrow. Then what?

In the impermanence that is our lives, the last thing we need to cling to is past tense. Wishing for something that is gone clogs our mind and clouds the joy and happiness that is desperately trying to get our attention. Wishing for past tense is "stinking thinking" in one of its purest forms—unwise, unskillful, and waste-filled. We deserve better.

Let's all agree to just let go. When it doesn't work, it just doesn't work.

There are simply times when you and I can give a relation-ship everything we've got and it doesn't matter. If a marriage isn't going to work, if our partner decides she hates us, we need to move on. Let past tense be past tense. Isadasi had to let go of more than anyone I know. She had to give up every hope of marriage. Any chance of having a permanent home. Yet in so doing, she discovered what really mattered to her: living a peace-filled life. As a side benefit, her search for peace led her to become one of the world's first enlightened women. Not a bad trade-off for three sucky marriages.

When It's Over, Move On

I was never a groupie. I actually think my mother worried about me as a teenager because I never hooked into any of the rock stars or young hunk actors or actresses, never plastered my walls with pin-up posters. Now, if author-entrepreneur-and-all-around-good-guy Paul Hawken had been around then, things might have been different, but he wasn't, so my walls stayed pristine.

Then, when I was a graduate student, it hit. I fell into a fantasy-driven, lust-filled, have-I-got-a-crush-on-you love with a young professor. I would even "audit" his classes (statistics—how sick is that?!) just to be around him. When one of my fellow students casually mentioned that he seemed to notice me I saw that as an omen from the gods that we were meant for each other. Not that we had ever spoken. After a week of sleepless nights and an inability to ingest any food of value I finally mustered the courage to plan a serendipitous encounter, casually mentioning that I had a crush on him and that I thought he might get a kick out of knowing.

The love affair began. Since fantasy isn't reality, I discovered I had a moody, angry, narcissistic lover on my hands, but who cared, the planets had put us together. Our relationship was shared karma. We were soul mates!

Then one morning he was gone. No warning.

I was a mess. At the time, I was working in Portland's city hall, as one of the "front faces" for the mayor's office. An information and referral specialist, people would call with basic questions and I would just sob into the telephone, which made it hard to understand the information I was giving them. Sometimes I would just sit at my desk working, as tears streamed down my face.

After about two weeks of nonstop weeping, my bosses had had enough. At the time, my mentor was a wonderful African American woman who was the chief lieutenant to one of the city's commissioners. I was continually in awe of her calmness under extreme pressure and all manner of crises. (Her boss was the police and fire commissioner, as I recall.) She always had a ready ear when I approached with questions about my work or casually asked for advice about life in general.

I found myself, trying desperately not to cry, facing her at a staff luncheon. When the lunch was over, she motioned to me to stay while everyone else left. Then she sat down next to me, locked eyes, and force fed me one of the best pieces of advice of my life: "What is with you white women?! When you get fucked over by a man you let them fuck you over and over in your heads. That would never happen to a black woman. If a man fucks us over he just does it once. Get over it." She was really angry at me. How dare I keep beating myself up over something that I had absolutely no control over?! What was wrong with me?! She was right. I sat there stunned. Then I followed her advice.

At first I just said "Let go!" to myself every time his name popped into my head. Then it was "Let go!" every time I heard one of "our" songs, until I just quit listening to the radio altogether. I put away any reminders of "us" until one morning, about a month after he had left, I didn't need to let go anymore. He was out of my head. My mind was clear again, it was a new day, and the sun was shining. A big fat lesson stared me right in the face when I came up for that first breath of sanity. Crazy wisdom is not about willpower, not about forcing anything. It is more like one of those Zen alarm clocks that gently gongs you awake, over and over, until you're up.

Years later, reading Kala and Capa's story for the first time, and remembering Patacara and Isadasi, I was able to see my own fantasies, my own delusions, my own seduction tactics back then and laugh. And I actually became friends with that old lover. Okay, not best friends, but it sure beats hoping to see his name in the obituaries, if you get my drift.

SURVIVING THE DEATH OF OUR LOVED ONES

Back to India 2,500 years ago. Patacara was such a beautiful young woman that her parents locked her in the seventh floor of their mansion and surrounded her with guards to prevent her from spending any time with men. In spite of their efforts, Patacara fell in love with one of the servants. One night, having decided that she couldn't live without him, she disguised herself as a servant and escaped with him to a different kingdom. There they managed to find and purchase a small plot of land where they farmed together.

Things went well until the young woman became pregnant. Knowing her husband would never go back to her parents' home in Savatthi, she decided to return to her mother alone— for help with the birth. Patacara never made it to her mother, giving birth to a baby boy along the road. Since she no longer had a reason for seeing her parents, Patacara returned to the farm.

When Patacara found herself pregnant a second time, once again she wanted to go to her parents' house to get some help with the birth. Her husband, sure he would be killed if her parents caught him, begged Patacara not to go. Not listening, she packed her things and started off, their son on her hip.

Her husband followed her, begging her to return to the farm.

About halfway to Savatthi, the three got caught in a terrible thunderstorm. To make matters worse, labor pains started. Patacara's husband frantically started to build a shelter for them on a nearby hill, only to be bitten by a poisonous snake. He fell down dead in the woods. In the meantime Patacara gave birth to a second son in the middle of the storm and waited through the night for her husband, terrified.

When he didn't return Patacara picked up her children and went looking for him. Almost immediately she spotted his dead body. Stunned with grief, Patacara decided to continue on to her parents' home. After walking for most of a day she reached the river, Aciravati. Because of the storm, the river was swollen and moving fast.

She knew she would never make it across carrying both boys. After thinking about her options, Patacara decided that she would leave her older son on the one bank and swim across with the baby. Reaching the other side she carefully set the baby in a natural nest on the bank. Starting back across the river to get to the other side, she heard a screech when she was about midstream. A hawk had spotted the baby and grabbed it in its talons. Terrified, Patacara screamed. The older boy, hearing her, thought she was calling to him. He stepped into the river only to be swept away by the current.

Half crazed by the loss of her beloved husband and two children, Patacara managed to make it to the outskirts of Savatthi only to be told by a fellow traveler that her parents' house had collapsed on them in the storm. They were also dead.

That was it. Patacara went wildly insane, tearing off her clothes and running around naked, screaming at the top of her lungs. Buddha, teaching nearby, heard, then spotted her. He immediately shouted, "Regain your mindfulness!" In that moment she stopped screaming and started weeping quietly. She told Buddha about all the relationships she had lost in the last day. He listened with great compassion, comforting her. In that moment she realized that she could get through anything. Even the loss of all of her loved ones.

In Buddha's presence, Patacara realized how impermanent everyone and everything is. She saw the universality of suffering. Cleansed of her madness, she decided to use her grief to feed her spiritual work. One of her great gifts to the rest of us is her personal enlightenment poem, a teaching that precisely describes the sequence of events that often take place just before realization or awakening:

> I've done everything right
> and followed the rule of my teacher
> I'm not lazy or proud.
> Why haven't I found peace?
>
> Bathing my feet
> I watched the bathwater
> spill down the slope.
> I concentrated my mind
> the way you train a good horse.
>
> Then I took a lamp
> and went into my cell,
> checked the bed,
> and sat down on it.
> I took a needle
> and pushed the wick down.
>
> When the lamp went out
> my mind was freed. [7]

The Impermanence of Everyone and Everything
Every thing and every person is impermanent. We will lose all of it when we die—our youth, our mate, our children, our family, and our friends. We will lose where we live, what we drive, our work, our books, and our favorite outfit. The sooner we admit to the loss, the easier our lives will become. We'll

stop sweating the small stuff for one thing. How important is a coffee stain on our favorite shirt compared to a last look at our best friend? Who cares if someone cuts us off on the highway when we compare that to never seeing our children again?

Acknowledging impermanence motivates us to sort through our lives, separating what matters from what doesn't. We see what is precious and at a minimum vow to be better caretakers of ourselves, our loved ones, and our environment. Junk gets cleared out—emotional, psychic, and physical. As it does, we find that we have more time and energy available for the important things, like spiritual work and helping other people.

For many of us, loss is accompanied by a period of intense concentration or prayer. Often this is fed by grief, sadness, and despair. At some point relaxation follows the concentrated effort. Then a sudden unexpected movement—a chair falling or door slamming or, in Patacara's case, a lamp suddenly going out—triggers awakening, the sudden certainty of our interconnectedness through time and space, the sudden sensation of being deeply comforted, content, and free from the tangles of our painful emotions.

Coming out of Our Pain

Then again, sometimes it helps to be shocked into letting go when we get stuck in our mourning or if our initial numbness doesn't dissipate over time. For Patacara it was Buddha shouting at her to get a grip. For one of my heartbreaks it was a counselor yelling at me that I was teaching my daughter to be a victim with all my whining. Bam! Suddenly I could let go of ten years of effort, of clinging to a one-of-us-needs-to-make-the-first-move-to-leave relationship. For some people, music can offer the shock. Loud country western, tears-in-our-beers songs. Or *The Mikado*. Or a raw—and I mean real raw—movie, like *Apocalypse Now*.

The death of someone we love cuts us off at the knees. We are shocked. We rage. We go crazy for a while. It's okay. These are all natural reactions. Healing happens over time if we allow ourselves to genuinely feel our emotions. And healing will happen at its own pace, no matter how much our friends and families wish we would speed things up because they hate to see us so raw. If we have the courage to simply be with our mourning, we'll be able to let go naturally—not of the memories but of the day-to-day patterns of the relationship that have been our home.

THE IMPORTANCE OF FRIENDS

Finally, there's this. Surviving the loss of a lover includes realizing how much you and I need each other. The ancient women created small communities where they offered each other silent, mindful acceptance and support. They prepared food for each other, made each other tea, sewed robes for each other. They defended and protected each other. Following their lead can help all of us to survive the loss of all our lovers. I've discovered that volunteering for a domestic violence program or working with a hospice or in a children's hospital ward can each nudge me into letting go and moving on when I'm really stuck. How dare I feel sorry for myself or waste any time plotting revenge when I have a roof over my head, food on my plate, clothes on my back? How dare you? We need to take care of each other. We need to remind each other to be grateful for what we do have. And to stop whining. This is dharma.

Sooner or later we all lose our lovers. Sometimes it's to someone else. Sometimes it's to his or her next lifetime.

Sometimes it's to a yearning so deep they can't give it up even though they try. Knowing this, our job is to be grateful for what we do have—our health, our breath, the people who stay in our lives. We need to expand this gratitude to include the flowers in our front yard, the birds in the sky, and the puppy down the street. In its expansion the gratitude becomes a special, sweet refuge, a place we can always return to since, when we look, we see that there is always something that merits gratitude. Even if it's simply our breath. Knowing that everything is impermanent we need to take good care of ourselves as well—so that when it's time to let go we'll be able to loosen our grip with a grace that would make Patacara proud.

Chapter Eight
THE GIFT OF BONE-DEEP LONELINESS

In the early 1970s I had awakened to the awareness that the conditions of my life were fundamentally connected to, affected by, and in part determined by the conditions experienced by all other women. That understanding made me want to grasp the total picture, that is, to discover the contours of the largest human/social/political pattern in which my own life operated. I saw myself not as an isolated individual but as part of a vast community of women with similar problems and goals, within a larger community of men, women and children throughout the world.

— SANDY BOUCHER, *Opening the Lotus*

LONELINESS HAPPENS. We may be surrounded by people right now, but at some point we won't be. Even when we think we have our bases covered, someone to care for us in our old age, an extended family nearby, and a condominium in an assisted living center, there are no guarantees that we will be able to escape loneliness. There are no guarantees for us, and there were no guarantees in Buddha's time.

FALLING INTO LONELINESS

Soma's life is one example of guarantees gone awry. The mother of ten children, we can only imagine how busy Soma was—after all, those were the days before television, cars, delivery services, and Amazon.com. Her entire adult life was spent birthing, nursing, and raising children, followed by educating them and finding spouses for them. So infamous was she that the whole city knew her as "Soma with many children."

Her husband started out as a pretty devoted spouse. Over time, unfortunately, he became less and less helpful, finally taking ordination as a monk. Although Soma was understandably upset by this, she didn't spend much time mourning—not that she had any time to mourn. At least with ten children she wasn't lonely.

As the kids grew up, Soma herself became increasingly devout. Once her youngest crossed the threshold of adulthood, she called all of her children together and announced that she wanted to split her considerable fortune among them. That way, no matter what happened to her, they and their families would always be financially secure. The only thing she asked for in return was a roof over her head, food on her plate, and clothes on her body—generosity unheard of during her time.

At first her children were good about taking care of their mother. But, over time, resentment surfaced. It was bad enough that their father had abandoned them to become an ascetic, now their mother was headed in the same direction. That was crazy. And who wanted to take care of a crazy old lady?

At first there were just problems in spots. A missed meal here, a disagreement over where she was supposed to be staying there. Finally, one by one, the children refused to take care of her, refused to let her stay with them.

Every possible emotion hit as Soma realized that she had been completely abandoned by her family. Waves of fury were followed by bitterness—forget pulling any arrow out. She had raised her children with the expectation that, in time, they would take care of her. Loneliness followed shock and anger, a bone-wearying loneliness that she had never expected to know. As soon as she was able to admit to herself that her entire family was abandoning her and that was just plain how her life was going to be, she joined the sangha of nuns.

At first she was just miserable there. The rules didn't match her lifelong habits. When Soma occasionally insisted on doing things her way, she found herself the victim of criticism and constant corrections—by much younger women no less.

In a fit of unhappiness she isolated herself from everyone. But the isolation just led to more loneliness. Deciding to just lean into the lonliness with every ounce of energy she could muster, Soma saw how much she had narrowed her definition of happiness over time. Her definition was that happiness was a product of being surrounded, and cared for, by her children. Since that was now out of the question, she would have to start looking at the whole world, beginning with the nuns, as a great dharma companion. Expectations had to go; so did judgment.

Having a mate or children never guarantees protection from loneliness. Even ordination as a nun, all by itself, cannot guarantee peace of heart. Her life was just as it was. No more, no less.

Soma became determined to use her loneliness as a springboard for enlightenment. She vowed to practice mindfulness with every waking breath. At the same time, she memorized any teaching that could help her counteract negative emotions when they arose. Then she threw herself into her spiritual practice. Because she was elderly, Soma knew that there wasn't much time left to her, so she would sit through the night in meditation. Sometimes she would do walking meditation outside of their living space so she wouldn't disturb the other nuns. Through such energetic effort, the elderly woman transformed her loneliness into a vehicle for her own enlightenment.

Soma's final spiritual breakthrough happened without warning, on an ordinary day, one where the other nuns had left her behind at the convent:

> Then the other bhikkunis
> Left me alone in the convent.
> They had given me instructions
> To boil a cauldron of water.
>
> Having fetched the water,
> I poured it into the cauldron;
> I put the cauldron on the stove and sat—
> Then my mind became composed.
>
> I saw the aggregates as impermanent,
> I saw them as suffering and nonself.
> Having expelled all the cankers from my heart,
> Right there I attained arahantship. [1]

When Buddha heard her news he recited a special verse in praise of Soma's effort:

> Though one should live a hundred years
> As a lazy, sluggish person,
> Better it is to live a single day
> Firmly arousing one's energy. [2]

In the most surprising actions, Soma found happiness. Fetching water, boiling it. Doing mundane chores. She threw herself into everything she did, concentrating on what was right in front of her. She completely accepted the fact that she was a little old lady living her life without her children. With the fusion of her mindfully spent days and her energetic effort, enlightenment, spurred on by loneliness.

Expanding Our Definition of Happiness

Too often we pigeonhole ourselves into specific roles—mom, spouse, teacher, student. The thing is, these change; we change. It is immeasurably more productive to decide what core things matter to us—spirituality, natural beauty, ethics, and so on—and move out from there. It is better to let our deepest values define what roles we play and when. If, for example, your deepest value is supporting a clean environment and we have just decided to demonstrate it by organizing a campaign against the city's incinerator, it is probably not an auspicious time to get pregnant. Rather than assume that our children will take care of us—assuming we have children at some point—better to downsize our needs and surroundings so that we can care for ourselves as long as possible.

One way to break free of roles is to think long and hard about what our deepest values are. From there we can survive and even enjoy shifting roles. Happiness happens when our lives are consistent with our values. By being kind, compassionate, sympathetic, and calm (deep values for many of us) we feed ourselves and the world. None of these behaviors depend on our having a particular role.

Use Your Loneliness

One of the surprise gifts of loneliness is the gift of time. Time gives us a chance to deepen our spiritual work. We actually have a half hour to pray or meditate or read scriptures. In the ensuing calmness, we can ask ourselves what needs doing so we won't feel lonely. What can we do that isn't dependent on a partner agreeing with our decision? We can volunteer, make new friends, write a poem or song. When we combine clarity about values with spiritual work, it is difficult to be lonely. Once the women in Buddha's time began to devote themselves to spiritual work, they didn't speak of loneliness again. There was no room for it.

In days filled with chores related to Still Point, a Zen Buddhist Temple located in the heart of Detroit, I can't imagine being lonely. Instead, I crave quiet time where I can simply sit in meditation, feeling its deep grounding and sweet energy. While I'm pleased to have company when I do, I'm as happy being alone. I expect that you'll find the same truth. The more you nurture who you really are, the less you'll need other people. Instead, you'll enjoy and cherish them when they are with you and enjoy the quiet of aloneness when they are not.

Some time ago I was asked to write an article about loneliness. As I thought about it I let myself do a quick scan of my own life. When have I been lonely? As a child, I was lonely whenever we moved. Not knowing anyone in the new place was pretty scary, and it was tough not having a friend's house for refuge when my sisters and I would begin punching each other to pass the time. I was lonely when I went off to college, traveling all the way from Sydney, Australia, then a small and even quaint city, to 110th and Amsterdam in New York City.

Though I was lonely on these occasions, I never expected to feel lonely when I was married, but I was sometimes. It didn't matter that I was married to a kind man, a man who said he loved me and meant it. In our first year of marriage we moved clear across the country, away from all my relatives and friends. I was so lonely sometimes that I even missed the fights with my sisters and lost count of how many times I dialed my mother's phone number to ask her if I could go home, hanging up just before she answered.

It is so hard to admit we're lonely. Most of us feel as if we've failed somehow, done something wrong. Coming from a family tradition skilled in denial (Irish, beer drinking; German, beer drinking) I ignored the loneliness for as long as I could and stayed as busy as possible, quilting and canning pears— and I didn't even like canned pears, but there was a pear tree behind our little house and karma is karma.

When loneliness would insist on rearing its confusing and scary head, and I couldn't ignore it any longer, I would read articles about it in magazines. I borrowed every book the Portland, Oregon, library had on the subject, so embarrassed that I hid the books between nature books by John McPhee. To this day, even though he is one of my favorite authors, I feel a sadness when I pick up his writing, because it reminds me of how lonely I once was.

A solution surfaced, two actually: I had a baby, and we got a dog. Both just made me busier and lonelier even though they were completely adorable. Back to the drawing board, I finally had the courage to face the dragon. I had finally named it but hadn't done more than that. Looking back, naming it was a big part of moving up and out of feeling lonely.

We spend a lot of time running away from difficult emotions, convinced that facing them will harm us more. While I've never known this to be true in the long run, at first, ouch. But then comes the freedom and an authenticity as to how to live our lives that I, for one, would never change. At every turn, Buddha's women disciples practiced leaning into their emotions. They were unwilling to waste their time on denial. Life was too short. It still is.

So I admitted to myself that I was lonely even though I had all the things I thought would protect me from loneliness—a wonderful husband, an adorable son, and an almost-trained puppy.

And I did a surprising thing for me at the time. I leaned right into it. Maybe it was the exhaustion of 3:00 A.M. feedings or the dog deciding that barking at 4:00 A.M. was his favorite thing. Whenever I felt lonely I just stared it in the face and let it take over. I just sat with it, curious in my own exhausted way, to see what would happen.

What happened was that it went away. The first time I stared it down, it took a couple of hours. The next time, about forty-five minutes. After that, mere minutes. Over a decade of meditation seems to have kept my emotional channels pretty clear. Now, even when I have a wave of loneliness, it is simply a cloud floating by, no big deal.

Years later I learned that I had tripped over a big deal Buddhist teaching: facing the emotional dragon that holds us back from our own awakening. If the dragon—named loneliness in this case—won't go away, we just need to ask it, politely of course, to open its mouth, because we're coming in. If you decide to try this, you'll find that the dragon immediately shrinks in size and the loneliness will become clear enough to address it. Sometimes, just looking at the dragon is all we need for it to disappear into the ether. Who would have guessed?

Maybe—surprise, surprise—facing our loneliness and using it as energy will shift us into awakeness. If it doesn't, at least we can keep leaning into it until we can peacefully get though our days in one piece.

From there, lots of things can happen. Because loneliness typically shows up when we are separated from people we love, deciding that everyone is our loved one can considerably shift the experience of loneliness. Buddha held that everyone has Buddha nature, that each of us is filled with a basic goodness that can be tapped for the benefit of others. While the news media may remind us that some people have lost their connection with their innate goodness, most people have not. Most of us try to be good. Most of us try to be kind. Most of us are instinctively helpful in a situation that needs us to be.

THE WORLD AS OUR NEIGHBORHOOD

When we acknowledge that everyone has this innate goodness, the whole world becomes our neighborhood and everyone in it our friend. One example of how powerful this understanding can be to the life of one person—not to mention everyone she met—is the story of Peace Pilgrim.

Mildred Lisette Norman was born in 1908 on a small chicken farm in Egg Harbor City, New Jersey. She was the oldest of three children in a household filled with extended family. A spunky kid, Mildred spent most summers exploring the local landscape, ultimately spending her days at a local watering hole when she wasn't practicing diving off the Moluka River Bridge.

A real clotheshorse, Mildred got a job as soon as she was old enough so she could buy better clothes than her family could afford. As soon as she graduated from high school she went to work full-time so she could save up for "a luxurious soft bed and a flashy car." She quickly married a man who also loved nice things. An entrepreneur, he started a trucking business that, given the economic depression of the time, didn't have a chance.

The two were known for their fights: "He would come home and make some announcement and she would exclaim, 'Oh, you imbecile!'" When her dad was killed in a car accident in 1936, Mildred's extended family, including several aunts who had nowhere else to go, moved in with her and her husband. Her marital relations slid from bad to worse. The couple moved to Philadelphia in 1939 in an effort to reestablish a solid base—both in their relationship and income—but by the time he joined the army to fight in World War II she had made it very clear that she had no interest in following him to his post.

Instead, Mildred stayed behind to work with senior citizens and people with emotional problems. Over time, she became more and more involved in the Women's International League for Peace and Freedom, gradually metamorphosing into a lobbyist for peace. At the same time, she had a realization that trying to live a self-centered life was meaningless. Worldly goods were burdens to her, not blessings. She adopted a life of voluntary simplicity.

Then, on January 1, 1953, Mildred, now calling herself Peace Pilgrim, vowed to remain "a wanderer until mankind has learned the way of peace." Walking alone, penniless, and with no organizational backing, Peace Pilgrim traveled on foot across the country, using her walking as an opportunity to inspire others to think about, and work for, peace. Her clothing was always the same, a navy blue shirt and pants, with a pocketed tunic over both. In the tunic's pockets she carried her only earthly possessions: a comb, a folding toothbrush, a ballpoint pen, copies of her message of peace, and her current correspondence.

By 1964, Peace Pilgrim had walked 25,000 miles. Deciding to stop counting and just walk, she began to make public presentations about peace. Everyone is capable of promoting peace, of being peace. Everyone is connected. She walked and spoke through the McCarthy era, the Korean War, and the Vietnam War. She talked on city streets and dusty roads, in ghettos, suburbs, deserts, and truck stops. Known for her contagious zest and ready wit, she was invited to speak at schools, universities, and churches. Peace Pilgrim traveled alone. In that aloneness she discovered a joy and gratitude that grew every day.

Peace Pilgrim walked alone through the most dangerous parts of the urban landscape. She slept beside the road, on beaches, in bus stations. She walked through all fifty states and the ten provinces of Canada. She walked through parts of Mexico as well. "I walk until given shelter, fast until given food. I don't ask—it is given without asking. Aren't people good! There is a spark of good in everybody, no matter how deeply it may be buried, it is there. It is waiting to govern your life gloriously." [3]

When she died, Peace Pilgrim was crossing the country for the seventh time.

Okay, maybe you and I can't be the Peace Pilgrim, but we can start seeing more people as our friends. Her experience of people was that we were all her friends, whether she knew us or not. If that is true, everyone gets a hello. And when everyone gets a hello, loneliness can't find a resting place.

Compassion toward Others

The whole world is our neighborhood. When a handful of us moved into the Still Point Abbey in Detroit, we were the only house on four corners in a neighborhood that sits somewhere between complete destruction and "just might turn around." If you look out our front window, you see a lone, boarded-up apartment building behind a vacant lot. Just behind the apartments are the sounds of the highway that sliced the neighborhood in two during one of the urban renewal frenzies of the last century. To our left is another huge vacant lot, backed by an apartment house where crack cocaine still has a tight grip. To our right, another house, then a vacant lot, then two big old brick houses that are imploding on themselves. "Not an obvious community," you'd say to yourself.

But the bus stop is right in front of the abbey, so I see the same handful of people getting on and off the bus every day. And I say hi, and if I'm picking up trash instead of heading for the car on an errand, I'll ask how the person is. For the first couple of weeks in the house I'm pretty sure people's reactions were to wish us away to anywhere else. But now, we chat. A couple sit on the porch when the weather is bad. One keeps a running grade on my house-painting skills (B- for the windowsills; C+ for the porch ceiling). They are my friends, these bus-riding buddhas, and I'm not even the least bit worried about being lonely.

Then there is this: Loneliness can't survive compassion for other people. When we focus on someone else's needs, we can't get caught up in obsessing about our own problems. There just isn't enough time in a day. And if we add to that compassion by getting involved in fun, heart-driven adventures, we're guaranteed a life filled with people who care about us back. Even if the projects are completely based on crazy wisdom. In fact, the crazier the projects, the more fun you'll have. Honest.

Crazy Wisdom

> CRAZY: Foolish, not sensible, very enthusiastic, eager
> WISDOM: The quality of being wise, good judgment, learning, knowledge

Crazy wisdom is a sure cure for loneliness because it creates connections with other people where you never thought any existed. In the middle of those connections is a wellspring of joy, often in the form of laughter. You decide to pick up the garbage in the park since nobody else seems to notice it. On exactly the same day, someone else is there picking up garbage. Catching each other's eye, all you can do is grin. You just have to meet each other. You discover that you have lots of values in common even though you are a middle-aged white woman and he is a young African American teenager. A new friend. Crazy wisdom.

Crazy wisdom is Betty Ashton Andrews deciding to take her harp down to the neonatal intensive care unit at Vanderbilt Medical Center in Nashville, Tennessee. There she plays her harp for several hours one day a week to relieve stress for the staff and the small patients. The result: a whole family of new friends.

Crazy wisdom is deciding to hang an expensive set of wind chimes on a tree in a tough neighborhood—low enough so anyone can grab it. That's where the temple's chimes hang. Their sound is so beautiful that sometimes people stop to just listen to them. The tree stands on a street of university students, crack addicts, aggressive homeless people, prostitutes, and a couple of monks. That the chimes are still there two years later reminds us that we are community, linked together by its sound.

Crazy wisdom is an entire country, Bhutan, deciding that measuring its national well-being with an economic statistic simply didn't make any sense. So it came up with a "gross happiness index," managing to protect more species of plants and animals—as a side effect—than the rest of world combined.

Crazy wisdom pushes loneliness right out of our system. Writ large, sometimes it even changes the lives of thousands of people, maybe more. In the competition for space in our minds, loneliness doesn't have a chance when we trip over something that can help other people in its creation.

BUILDING COMMUNITIES THROUGH CRAZY WISDOM

In 1972, after the war of independence, Muhamad Yunus, a young economist, traveled from the United States to his home in Bangladesh to see what he could do to help rebuild the infrastructure of his country. After a short stint as a bureaucrat, he became the chairman of the Economics Department at Chittagong University. Because the university cut through a small village, he got to know people in the community. One was a beggar named Sufiya, who was the second wife of a man who had died in the 1950s leaving her with seven children to raise. All but two had died. When Yunus met Sufiya she was trying to earn money by weaving bamboo stools to sell. The only problem was that she couldn't earn enough profit to buy supplies. So she would work for a while. Then beg. Then work. Yunus and his students lent her the money she needed to buy material for more stools, enough to actually earn her a living. The amount of the loan? A couple of dollars. She was so successful that they made a couple more loans, and the idea for a bank was born.

In the last twenty years the Gameen Bank has made loans worth more than $1.5 billion to people all the rest of us had pretty much written off as doomed to poverty—landless villagers in Bangladesh. Because its loans are tiny in comparison with other financial institutions, the bank has more than two million clients, 94 percent of whom are women. Ninety-seven percent of the loans are repaid, one of the highest repayment rates in the industry. This is an extraordinary rate given that the interest rates for the loans have been known to go as high as 16 percent. Because of the hours it takes to work with the borrowers, the bank usually needs to charge interest rates that are three or four points above the going commercial rate. It never forgives loans. There can be a flood, a fire, a plague, a cyclone—doesn't matter. Plus, fees are charged for everything it gives to the borrowers, from assistance with paperwork to packets of new vegetable seeds.

Unlike other banks—maybe even all other banks—Gameen only lends in villages. The women don't get loans by demonstrating credit history, because they have none. And they don't have to furnish collateral—something that could be sold if they default on their loan—because they typically don't own anything worth the amount of the loan. The women aren't even asked to find someone who will guarantee the loan, because the bankers know there isn't anyone.

Instead, each borrower has to join a five-person group, attend weekly training and support meetings, and take responsibility not only for her own loan but for the whole group! It works. Because of their mutual responsibility, the groups are very careful about letting any new entrepreneurs into the fold—if one woman defaults they are all in trouble. On the other hand, if all five repay the loans, they are each guaranteed access to credit for the rest of their lives.

When Yunus came up with the idea for the bank, he was laughed out of so many offices that he didn't bother to keep count. His idea was too wacky. With nothing to lose, he kept going. At the same time, communities of women formed around the concept, supporting and encouraging him. They became a community of friends. The money started to come, until today millions of villagers now have enough food every day and clothing. The women are buying medicine, paying for their children's educations and weddings so they can have positive starts to their adult years.

His was crazy wisdom: an idea that didn't make rational sense when it was first introduced. Lending money to beggars?! Never forgiving loans?! And yet, both worked so well that Gameen has become a model for community-based economic development around the world.

REFUSE TO ISOLATE YOURSELF

For a long time I was pretty isolated as a management consultant, and for good reason. I tended to love working with the clients who did not make my firm any money—nonprofit organizations and start-up companies. Instead of developing complicated or sophisticated processes, I'd plead with executive directors and chief executive officers to keep things as simple as possible for as long as they could stand it: to get to know their customers as intimately as they legally and ethically could; to grow their companies slowly—advice that felt almost anti-American even as the words came out of my mouth.

After five years it was clear to me and my partners that I needed to leave the firm—we just weren't a match. The firm's overhead costs couldn't carry my feed-the-world billing pattern.

So I left and started to train people to start and build businesses that began with an investigation of one's deepest values and moved out from there. I figured that once entrepreneurs were clear about what mattered to them they could come up with product ideas, rather than the other way around (which is the typical way people start businesses). To kick-start the training, I designed a workshop series called "Building a Business the Zen Way." I figured that in a town of 100,000, a dozen people might sign up. Over a hundred people did. We didn't have space for everyone. And when the first classes ended the participants refused to stop meeting, creating a support community that continues to meet years later.

Creating the program, teaching the classes, and meeting with the entrepreneurs after the training ended protected me from the worst possible professional loneliness—isolation. I made great friends, people I enjoy to this day. I learned as much as I taught. And if I ever start to feel a wave of loneliness in the future I can always pull out the book and teach another set of classes, for free next time. I'll aim it at teenage moms.

I refused to isolate myself and gave myself permission to try on my own brand of crazy wisdom. It worked out because wisdom does. And it taught me the value of listening to crazy ideas instead of writing them off as fantasy.

LONELINESS IS JUST LONELINESS

There is a wonderful story about a young monk who begs a Zen master to let him become one of his students. The Zen master responds that he will let him stay in his temple if the young monk can cook rice well.

No problem.

The young monk, graduate of the best culinary institute in China, quickly makes the master a pot of rice.

"Too hard!"

The master throws it on the ground and tells the monk to try again. A little bit disconcerted but willing to write the experience off as a bad day, the monk makes a second pot of rice.

"Too soft!"

Dumped on the ground again. The young monk heads back to the temple kitchen determined to show the master that he knows how to cook rice. The next batch will be the best rice he's ever had.

"Too watery!"

By the fourth round the young monk is a little desperate. He can't believe the rice isn't perfect, can't understand the rejection.

"Too dry!"

By now the young monk is in tears. Completely desperate, he does everything in slow motion to make certain that the rice is made according to the master's own recipe.

"Too soft!"

Nine times the master rejects the young monk's rice. Going

back for the tenth time, pot in hand, the young monk tells himself that this time the master's response doesn't matter. No big deal. He'll just keep making rice for the old man until he gets it right. If it takes a hundred times, okay. A thousand times? Okay.

Taking the pot to the master he starts to throw it onto the ground himself to save the master the trouble. Suddenly he feels a gentle pressure on his arm, stopping his movement.

"Perfect."

The trick to facing loneliness is to decide that loneliness is no big deal. We all get lonely sometimes. It's just a part of life. Our only job is to name it, lean into it, and then let it go. What does it take to let go? I vote that we let ourselves get so miserable that we are willing to try just about anything to get through it. In that space we'll find a spiritual energy that will take us to the next step. Maybe we just need to train our puppy minds not to wallow in the loneliness. Whenever the obsessing starts, we can literally say to ourselves "Let go." When I feel myself getting a little stuck in the land of lonely, I say the words out loud: "P'arang, let go." I've had friends write the words on the back of their hands. After a while our brains give in and we really can let go. We can focus on some-thing else, we can be crazy in a way that feeds the world a little more compassion.

Then, when loneliness just has to check in every once in a while to see if we still have a place for it, we can give it per-mission for a quick, loving visit, but then, adios amigo. We have some crazy wisdom to attend to.

If nothing else works, becoming a monastic helps. There's always room at the abbey for one more Buddha.

Chapter Nine
ALONENESS

MEDITATION ON ALONENESS

Settle yourself in a comfortable posture and allow your whole body to relax . . . When you feel connected with a climate of calmness and stillness within bring into your awareness a vision of yourself standing alone atop a high hill. . . .

As you see yourself standing on the hilltop let your awareness deepen, become more subtle. Feel the life around you, beneath you, above you. The movements of the trees and the clouds, the shadows on the hillsides, the endless changes which signal life, rising and passing. Feel the same changes within you, the rising and passing of your own thoughts and feelings. . . . Open yourself to feeling the transparency of the lines between inner and outer, self and other. Feel the transparency of the lines between aloneness and oneness. . . . Allow the love and compassion of oneness to fill your being.

—CHRISTINA FELDMAN, *Women Awake*

SOMEONE ONCE TOLD ME THAT 90 percent of all women will be alone for a significant portion of their adult life. For some of us it will be because we stay single all our lives. For others, serial monogamy will leave quiet times in between our relationships. Maybe we will marry and then divorce or become a widow. Knowing this, why do we cling so hard to relationships? They all end.

Knowing this, it is in our self-interest to see aloneness as an opportunity for genuine spiritual growth, a trigger for enlightenment even. That's what Buddha's women disciples did.

WE CAN'T DEPEND ON RELATIONSHIPS

So many of the women who followed Buddha were beautiful. In different ways they each discovered that beauty is fleeting and that it does not bring happiness. Khema, a woman from the elite class, was said to be so lovely that her skin was like pure gold. She was King Bimbisara's favorite lover. As such, she was spoiled, arrogant, and self-centered. When Buddha first appeared in her life she was not the slightest bit interested in what he had to say. Her life was working just fine, thank you very much.

But aging was inevitable, and beauty is impermanent. Relationships change, especially love affairs with kings. Sooner or later Khema was going to face being alone. And she was going to lose all of the things that were spoiling her. The fall was going to be a big one, steep and fast.

For a long time Khema resisted even being around Buddha's monks and nuns. But King Bimbisara, a follower of Buddha, was so determined to introduce the two that he hired a chorus of singers to sing songs praising the beauty and peacefulness of Veluvana, the monastery where the Buddha was living. He knew that Khema's love for beautiful surroundings would get the best of her. She would be too curious, would have to see the place for herself.

He was right. Khema couldn't bear to not see the hermitage.

When she arrived at Veluvana, it was as advertised. The whole place glowed, from the trees to the gardens. One of the nuns who showed her around suggested that, since she was already there, she might as well check out Buddha. So she did.

He changed her life in an instant. As Khema walked toward him he created a vision in front of her. It was of a woman even more beautiful than she. Shocked, Khema could only stare. Then she thought to herself, "Never before have I seen such a woman! I myself do not come within even a fraction of her beauty. Surely those who say the ascetic Gotama disparaged beauty of form must be misrepresenting him." [1] Then, right before her eyes, the woman in the vision shifted from a beautiful young woman to an attractive middle-aged woman to a gray-haired elderly woman with broken teeth and wrinkled skin. Then, if that wasn't bad enough, she fell to the ground, dead.

Khema was stunned. In a flash she saw how fleeting youth and beauty really are. We all lose them. Watching her reaction, Buddha told her that people who were attached to physical beauty, theirs or others', were bound to the world with all its heartbreak. On the other hand, those who could stay detached from such things, who could give up clinging to things that are impermanent, had great freedom. These were the ones whose identity and self-worth remained unfettered by their looks or the looks of others:

> Khema, behold this mass of elements,
> Diseased, impure, decaying;
> Trickling all over and oozing,
> It is desired only by fools . . .

Those enslaved by lust
drift down the stream
As a spider glides on its self spun web.
Having cut off even this, the wise wander
Indifferent to the pleasures they've renounced. [2]

His were turning words. Hearing them, Khema left the king and became not only a nun but one of the key teachers of the sangha. Even royalty showed up for her teachings.

To mark her shift, Khema wrote a poem, raw though it was. In it she talks about how she was pressured by society to be seduced by her own beauty, but finally understanding the transitory nature of beauty, she broke away:

(Man)
Come on, Khema!
Both of us are young.
And you are beautiful.
Let's enjoy each other!
It will be like the music
of a symphony.

(Khema)
I'm disgusted by this body.
It's foul and diseased.
It torments me.
Your desire for sex
means nothing to me.

Pleasures of the senses are
swords and stakes.

The elements of mind and body
are a chopping block for them.
What you call delight
is not delight for me.

Everywhere the love of pleasure
is destroyed,
the great dark
is torn apart.
And Death,
you too are destroyed.
Fools,
who don't know things
as they really are,
revere the mansions of the moon
and tend the fire in the wood
thinking this is purity.

But for myself,
I honor The Enlightened One
the best of all
and, participating in his teaching,
am completely freed from suffering. [3]

Buddha ended up naming Khema as one of his two foremost
disciples among the nuns. She was known for her wisdom.
There is a story in the *Samyutta Nikaya* in which she teaches
King Pasenadi about Buddhism. The king has stopped in a
small town in the kingdom of Kosala for the night. He asks his
attendants if they can find a monk to teach him, and they
come back with Khema.

Once he recovers from his shock, Pasenadi proceeds to discover a woman so disinterested in her own beauty that he is glued to her teachings. What is it that has given her such freedom? He learns that it is her willingness to let go, to live her own life, her own path. To live her life alone.

Khema so impresses the king that he ends up asking her a question that has been keeping him awake at night, namely, whether or not a Buddha exists after death. Khema gives him a terrific answer. Basically, she tells him that Buddhas are completely free from being defined by form, feeling, perception, volition, and consciousness, which means that the king's question doesn't make sense to ask, sort of like trying to count the grains of sand contained in the River Ganges. What would be the point? When King Pasenadi later asks Buddha the same question, he answers with exactly the same words.

Live Your Own Life

When we finally realize that we can't depend on impermanent things—beauty, youth, relationships—for our happiness, we have a choice to make. Will we wallow in what used to be, or will we see impermanence as providing us with a huge gateway to an independent life? I pick choice two. It offers each of us a life where we appreciate, where every day is filled with possibilities. Maybe today will be the day when the daffodils start to peek out of the ground. Maybe today I'll shave my head and give in to being a monk once and for all. When we let go of clinging to who we think we should be, or who we were, we can finally see how terrific we really are. You and I are fun. We care about people. We care about our world. We want to be happy. We have wonderful senses of humor and know how to laugh.

An independent life, one where we get to be what we truly

are, gives us freedom for all these things. If we happen to have partners, we can share them; if we don't, we get them all to ourselves—the laughter and delight, the surprise and appreciation, the hilarity of a new permanent that makes us look exactly like the Little Prince. When we learn about being alone and see it as a full life—not an empty one—our fears of being alone dissipate. If we don't want to be alone, we can always make a cake and give it to a stranger, just because. We can volunteer at the recycling center. We can make real friends on the Internet. We can pray for the world. We can even talk to our dead sister.

Living our own life is the point of genuine spiritual work. It is where awakening happens. When we are completely authentic, growth happens, spiritual efforts mature, and the events in our lives start to make complete sense—why we're with who we are with or why we're alone.

ALONENESS ON OUR SPIRITUAL PATH

For twelve years, from 1976 to 1988, Tenzin Palmo lived in a remote cave 13,200 feet up in the Himalayas. She was almost completely cut off from the world by the mountains and the snow. Her cave was nothing more than an overhang on a natural ledge of the mountain. Three sides were open to the elements. The cave itself was tiny, a small ten-by-six-foot room. You would have to stoop to get inside, and stay stooped. Her furnishings consisted of a wood-burning stove, a small table, a small bookcase with cloth-wrapped textbooks, and a meditation box. No bed. Just beyond the ledge? A sheer drop into the Lahouli Valley.

Staying there was no big deal, according to Palmo. Being totally alone was okay. Joy was there, and spaciousness.

Tenzin, born Diane Perry, had lots of suitors as a young

woman. At least three proposals of marriage followed her to Tibet. Hadn't she wished for a partner, marriage, or children in all those years? "That would have been a disaster. . . . It wasn't my path at all. . . . I was very happy [in the cave] and had everything I wanted. . . . I was never lonely, not for a minute. It was nice if someone visited. But I was perfectly happy not seeing anybody." [4]

Living alone gave Tenzin Palmo the time she needed to clean herself out and settle into powerful spiritual practice: "One evening I looked inside and saw this grasping and attachment and how much suffering it was causing me. Seeing it so nakedly at that moment it all fell away. From that moment on I didn't need to reach out. . . . There's no doubt that the West is obsessed with sex, thinks that you can't live without it and that, if you do, it's going to make you all warped and thwarted. It's absurd! Some of the most glowing and fulfilled people I've met have been chaste." [5]

Over and over, when Tenzin talks about her experience of aloneness she talks about how happy she was and how filled she was with joy as a cave dweller. She realized that there was nowhere else she wanted to be, nothing else she wanted to do, and she was filled with gratitude.

Tenzin is a wonderful role model for the rest of us because she is so clearheaded about the joy of aloneness. She teaches us that it is a gift because it allows us to jump-start our spiritual work in a deep and meaningful way. If we start and end our days with spiritual practice—even if it is five minutes of sitting, chanting, reading, or praying—we'll find our days taking on a slower, sweeter rhythm. And we'll want more of that. Without realizing it we'll start cleaning out the negative things in our lives—the people and associations—that don't feed us spiritually. We'll find ourselves wanting more quiet for reading, thinking, and simply being present. Over time, the sweetness can take over our days if we let it. And we'll realize that we are happy right where we are, whatever we are doing. We'll clean up the remaining gunk of our relationships, keep the good memories, spit out the bad. We'll find our own path once and for all and live happily ever after.

Finding Joy in Aloneness

Aloneness is not the same as loneliness. When we are lonely, we are unhappy to be alone. Aloneness is simply about being apart from other people, or, according to good old *Websters*, "without any other person." Unhappiness is not implied.

When we find that place of gratitude and joy in living a life alone, all sorts of doors start to open for us. It may be a new job. Or a new home. Maybe we'll literally open our doors to other spiritual seekers since we have too much space anyway. I guarantee that you'll laugh more.

And the more aloneness, the more shifting. Who knows, you might even become a revolutionary. Many women do. Years alone have a way of leading us toward our own . . . suchness. In other words, we have the opportunity to grow into who we are really meant to be. With eyes undistracted by family obligations, our energy can be turned to other things. Our passions are able to blossom. Without needing a partner's approval for the choices we make in how we spend our days, who knows what can happen?

Hildegard of Bingen lived eight hundred years ago. She spent huge chunks of time alone, in prayer. As her gratitude and joy grew, so did her wisdom and fearlessness. Over time, Hildegard became an adviser to bishops, archbishops, and emperors. She became a rabid advocate of better conditions in the monasteries and was so well regarded by everyone that she was called on all hours of the day for advice regarding unsolvable problems.

Women who are comfortable being alone aren't afraid to make choices that are good for them. They aren't afraid to demand a life that is meaningful. They know when their lives have meaning and when they don't. While they may care about the opinions of others, these are the women who are willing to pay the cost of unpopularity, to "follow their bliss," as Joseph Campbell has said, whatever it ends up being. Forget prescribed paths, they say.

FREEDOM THROUGH ALONENESS

In Buddha's time, Citta was a revolutionary. Word has it that before Buddha's lifetime she was—don't laugh—a fairy. When she wasn't flitting about, dropping fairy dust on plants, flowers, and people, she was thinking about becoming fully enlightened. Then, when she and Buddha managed to be born at around the same time, she was born into a wealthy family in Rajagaha. This allowed her some freedom to do spiritual practice, but family, friends, and social obligations kept her pretty busy until she was an old woman. Then, finally alone, she decided that she was no longer willing to compromise how she spent her days. Buddha's stepmother, Mahaprajapati, also a little old lady by that point, ordained her as a nun.

Citta decided that the best place to meditate was a place called Vulture's Peak, one of Buddha's favorite haunts. Climbing it slowly, step by step, she made it to the top. Sitting there, high above everyday life, finally, after so many lifetimes, she became enlightened:

Though I be suffering and weak, and all
My youthful spring be gone, yet have I climbed,
Leaning upon my staff, the mountain
crest.
Thrown from my shoulder hangs my
cloak, o'er-turned
My little bowl. So 'gainst the rock I lean
And prop this self of me, and break away
The wildering gloom that long had closed
me in. [6]

What Citta discovered in her aloneness was the freedom to nurture her deepest hunger, her spiritual work. Instead of feeling unhappy with the loss of family, friends, and social obligations, she embraced the changes in her life. Finally she could do the spiritual work she wanted to do, at her own pace. The reward? Immeasurable happiness.

Embrace Being Alone

Aloneness gives us the time we need to write, or to buy that motorcycle, or to finally take that painting class. One of my family's favorite stories is the story of my grandmother's tea-drinking mother, grandmother Willis. She gave her life to her husband, her children, and grandchildren until she was quite elderly. Finally, she was living alone, with no one to care for and no one to care for her. The whole extended family was worried about her. How would she spend her days? Would she die of loneliness? Maybe she would remarry. After all, she was still beautiful. If she didn't, how could they keep her busy? Should she live with one of the kids? She would have none of it. All her life she had been what everyone else wanted her to be, done what everyone else wanted her to do. No more. One day, with no warning, she put on a pair of fishnet stockings, high heels, one of her best dresses, and red lipstick and headed for the neighborhood bar, where she became a local icon. Always good company, always funny, sometimes tipsy, she was her most wonderful, having rejected the entire family's notion of her appropriate role. Best of all, she was really happy. Talk about a revolution.

As my mother moves toward seventy, I'm watching her open up as well. True to herself, a writer's writer, she is sharing more, writing wildly, and, finally, publishing. Down in their pool hall she is taking on all the retirees at the senior center. Usually she wins. She teaches an art class to seniors—just because. She has time to be angry about the social injustice in the world and to obsess about the state of the earth. When she is in love, she is in love and quite open about it. And when she isn't, she isn't. No big deal. People want to be near her energy and tenacious ways, even as she rants about one more "stupid" policy decision by a government that gets better and better at harming women and children. I want to be her when I grow up.

When we embrace aloneness, when we decide to be the protagonist in our own stories, the world breaks open for us. We can frame each day as its own precious picture, shrug off most of the irritations that come along, and discover a deep well of compassion that may be what saves the world in the end.

Space for Our Spiritual Work
Then there is this: In aloneness is the space and time we need for our spiritual work. Enlightenment can be ours. It's enough to make a woman laugh out loud, this upside down gift. Whoever would have thought, in a society that demands that

we singletons constantly search for mates, that being alone offers so much possibility? And so many gifts. Whoever would have thought that being alone could be a proactive life choice, and not a curse?

We all need to remember how wonderful it can be to be alone, or to learn it for the first time. Because aloneness will come. Patacara had to learn it. So did Capa. Kisagotami. All of the women who followed Buddha after a relationship.

So, woman, when you find yourself living alone, and statistics say all of us will at some point, embrace it. In your aloneness you may just find yourself falling in love with the whole world and everyone and everything in it. Maybe you'll end up breaking hearts in a Boston bar, or maybe you'll picket. Maybe you'll write letters to children desperate for love, or give yourself permission to, finally, eat popcorn in bed. The possibilities are endless. And if you do meet a special person to love, when you are able to embrace aloneness, then you will also be able to have a love relationship that is a true partnership.

> The day my Great-grandmother Willis turned sixty-five
> she decided she would spend the rest of her life
> wearing fishnet stockings and red lipstick.
>
> Her place of dwelling became Big Larry's sports pub
> not because she liked to drink
> but because she was simply aware of the fact
> that the world's most interesting people flocked to Big Larry's
> like seagulls flock to the dump.
> What she didn't know

is that it was she who compelled them.
That in the hearts located directly above Boston's
biggest beerbellies
she took precedence over all things
bottled or draft.

It was she who taught the women of my family
how to grow old
the Willis way.

Now
her daughter, my grandmother
is sixty-five
and enrolling in ballroom roller skating classes.

She has become the old lady
she beats the Urkel-pants'd old men in the pool hall,
while discussing George W. Bush
and how his presidency
will bring about the next apocalypse.

She is the old lady who paints pictures of Jesus on the
cross
with money seeping out of his open wounds.
All the while fulfilling her lifelong dream
of becoming a fashion photographer.

She is the old lady who turned her one-bedroom apartment
into a homeless shelter.

And as my grandmother becomes a great-grandmother
to multiple great-grandchildren
my mother will grow old, remember her Willis roots
and get sudden urges to dye her hair fuchsia
and buy a vintage Cadillac.
And as she reaches sixty-five
her vocabulary will consist solely of the phrase
"You go, girl!"

Around this time my doctor will tell me
I'm pre-menopausal
because apparently it runs in the family.

And I'll buy myself a cake
and imagine myself on my sixty-fifth birthday:
streaking across the White House lawn, yelling "Save
the Whales!"
with organic red lipstick
smeared across my shriveled little face
as I pull a bottle of malt liquor from my fishnet stockings
and toast my Great-grandmother Willis:
"You go, girl!"

—Jamie Markus, age eighteen,
"Growing Old the Willis Way"

May all beings be free.

NOTES

Chapter One
THE ANCIENTS

1. Hammalawa Saddhatissa, *Before He Was Buddha: The Life of Siddhartha* (Berkeley, Calif.: Seastone, 1998), p. 26.

2. H. W. Schumann, *The Historical Buddha: The Times, Life, and Teachings of the Founder of Buddhism*, trans. M. O'C. Walshe (London: Arkana, 1989), p. 116.

3. Nyanaponika Thera and Hellmuth Hecker, *Great Disciples of the Buddha: Their Lives, Their Works, Their Legacy* (Somerville, Mass.: Wisdom Publications, 1997), p. 154.

4. Ibid., p. 155.

5. Ibid., p. 155.

6. Ibid., p. 155.

7. C. A. F. Rhys Davids and K. R. Norman, trans., *Poems of the Early Buddhist Nuns* (Oxford: The Pali Text Society, [1971] 1977), p. 73.

Chapter Two
RELATIONSHIPS AS PARTNERSHIPS

1. Laura Kipnis, "Against Love: A Treatise on the Tyranny of Love," *New York Times Magazine*, October 14, 2001, p. 102.

2. Schumann, *The Historical Buddha*, p. 89.

3. Thera and Hecker, *Great Disciples of the Buddha*, pp. 300–301.

4. Ibid., pp. 301–303

5. Thich Nhat Hanh, *Touching Peace: Practicing the Art of Mindful Living* (Berkeley, Calif.: Parallax Press, 1992), pp. 50–52.

6. Geri Larkin, *The Still Point Dhammapada*, unpublished, Chapter 16.

7. Darlene Cohen, *Being Bodies: Buddhist Women on the Paradox of Embodiment* (Boston: Shambhala Publications, 1997), p. 15.

8. Beth Stone as told to Sara Ivry, *New York Times Magazine*, October 14, 2001, p. 132.

9. Ibid.

Chapter Three
RELATIONSHIP RAGE

1. Thera and Hecker, *Great Disciples of the Buddha*, p. 257.

2. Ranjini Obeyesekere, trans., *Portraits of Buddhist Women: Stories from the Saddharmaratnavaliya* (Albany: State University of New York Press, 2001), p. 162.

3. Ibid.

4. Ibid.

5. Ibid., p. 163.

6. Thera and Hecker, *Great Disciples of the Buddha*, p. 262.

7. Valerie Latona, "Give Up Your Grudge," *Natural Health*, July/August 2000, pp. 75–76.

8. Susan Murcott, *The First Buddhist Women: Translations and Commentaries on the Therigatha* (Berkeley, Calif.: Parallax Press, 1991), p. 64.

Chapter Four
JEALOUSY

1. *Webster's New World Dictionary of the American Language* (New York: The World Publishing Company, 1973).

2. Murcott, *The First Buddhist Women*, p. 98.

3. Obeyesekere, trans., *Portraits of Buddhist Women*, pp. 48–49.

4. Ibid., p. 8.

5. Thera and Hecker, *Great Disciples of the Buddha*, p. 304.

6. Ibid., p. 305.

7. Saddhatissa, *Before He Was Buddha*, p. 42.

8. Ibid., p. 42.

9. Ibid., p. 43.

10. Ibid., p. 43.

11. Ibid., p. 44.

12. Ibid., p. 44.

13. Ibid., p. 45.

Chapter Five
OUTSMARTING THE PULL OF AN AFFAIR

1. I. B. Horner, *Women under Primitive Buddhism: Laywomen and Almswomen* (Delhi: Motilal Banarsidass Publishers, 1930), p. 43.

2. Ibid., pp. 64–65.

3. Murcott, *The First Buddhist Women*, p. 124.

4. Ibid., pp. 126–27.

5. Horner, *Women Under Primitive Buddhism*, p. 59.

6. Thera and Hecker, *Great Disciples of the Buddha*, p. 284.

7. Ibid.

8. Horner, *Women under Primitive Buddhism*, p. 258.

9. Ibid., p. 283.

10. Thera and Hecker, *Great Disciples of the Buddha*, p. 307.

11. Ibid., p. 308.

Chapter Six
COMPETITION FOR OUR MATE

1. William Cash, *The Third Woman: The Secret Passion That Inspired the End of the Affair* (New York: Carroll & Graf, 2000), p. 3.

2. Ibid., p. 13.

3. Murcott, *The First Buddhist Women*, p. 87.

4. bell hooks, *All about Love: New Visions* (New York: William Morrow and Company, 2000), p. 139.

5. Joanna Macy, *World as Lover, World as Self* (Berkeley, Calif.: Parallax Press, 1991).

6. Jeff Greenwald, *Shopping for Buddhas* (San Francisco: Harper and Row, 1990), p. 50.

Chapter Seven
SURVIVING THE LOSS OF A LOVER

1. "Dumped: Get Mad? Get Even? No—Get Over Him!," *Glamour*, February 1999, p. 132.

2. Ibid.

3. Murcott, *The First Buddhist Women*, pp. 108–11.

4. Bhikkhu Bodhi, *The Connected Discourses of the Buddha: A New Translation of the Samyutta* Nikaya (Somerville, Mass.: Wisdom Publications, 2000), p. 180.

5. Thera and Hecker, *Great Disciples of the Buddha*, p. 311.

6. Murcott, *The First Buddhist Women*, p. 94.

7. Murcott, *The First Buddhist Women*, p. 34.

Chapter Eight
THE GIFT OF BONE-DEEP LONELINESS

1. Thera and Hecker, *Great Disciples of the Buddha*, p. 281.

2. Ibid., p. 281.

3. www.peacepilgrim.net

Chapter Nine
ALONENESS

1. Thera and Hecker, *Great Disciples of the Buddha*, p. 264.

2. Thomas Byrom, *Dhammapada: The Sayings of the Buddha* (Boston: Shambhala, 1993) p. 19.

3. Murcott, *The First Buddhist Women*, pp. 65–66.

4. Vicki Mackenzie, *Cave in the Snow: Tenzin Palmo's Quest for Enlightenment* (London: Bloomsbury Publishing, 1998), p. 4.

5. Ibid., pp. 53 and 185.

6. Davids and Norman, trans. *Poems of the Early Buddhist Nuns*, p. 21.

BIBLIOGRAPHY

Bhikkhu Bodhi. *The Connected Discourses of the Buddha: A New Translation of the Samyutta Nikaya.* Somerville, Mass.: Wisdom Publications, 2000.

Cash, William. *The Third Woman: The Secret Passion That Inspired the End of the Affair.* New York: Carroll & Graf, 2000.

Cohen, Darlene. *Being Bodies: Buddhist Women on the Paradox of Embodiment.* Boston: Shambhala Publications, 1997.

Davids, C. A. F. Rhys and K. R. Norman, trans. *Poems of the Early Buddhist Nuns.* Oxford: The Pali Text Society, [1971] 1977.

Feldman, Christina. *Woman Awake: A Celebration of Women's Wisdom.* London and New York: Penguin Arkana, 1990.

Gallant, China. *The Bond between Women: A Journey of Fierce Compassion.* New York: Riverhead Books, 1998.

Greenwald, Jeff. *Shopping for Buddhas.* San Francisco: Harper and Row, 1990.

Hanh, Thich Nhat. *Touching Peace: Practicing the Art of Mindful Living.* Berkeley, Calif.: Parallax Press, 1992.

hooks, bell. *All about Love: New Visions.* New York: William Morrow and Company, 2000.

Horner, I. B. *Women in Early Buddhist Literature.* Sri Lanka: Buddhist Publication Society, 1982.

Horner, I. B. *Women under Primitive Buddhism: Laywomen and Almswomen.* Delhi: Motilal Banarsidass Publishers, 1930.

Kipnis, Laura. "Against Love: A Treatise on the Tyranny of Love." *New York Times Magazine* (October 14, 2001): 102.

Larkin, Geri. *First You Shave Your Head.* Berkely, Calif.: Celestial Arts, 2001.

Larkin, Geri. "The Still Point Dhammapada." Still Point Zen Buddhist Temple, Detroit, 2002.

Latona, Valerie. "Give Up Your Grudge." *Natural Health* (July/August 2000): 75–76.

Lopes, Donald S. J. *The Story of Buddhism: A Concise Guide to Its History and Teachings.* San Francisco: Harper San Francisco, 2001.

Mackenzie, Vicki. *Cave in the Snow: Tenzin Palmo's Quest for Enlightenment.* London: Bloomsbury Publishing, 1998.

Macy, Joanna. *World as Lover, World as Self.* Berkeley, Calif.: Parallax Press, 1991.

Murcott, Susan. *The First Buddhist Women: Translations and Commentaries on the Therigatha.* Berkeley, Calif.: Parallax Press, 1991.

Obeyesekere, Ranjini, trans. *Portraits of Buddhist Women: Stories from the Saddharmaratnavaliya.* Albany: State University of New York Press, 2001.

Saddhatissa, Hammalawa. *Before He Was Buddha: The Life of Siddhartha.* Berkeley,Calif.: Seastone, 1998.

Schumann, H. W. *The Historical Buddha: The Times, Life, and Teachings of the Founder of Buddhism,* trans. M. O'C. Walshe. London: Arkana, 1989.

Thera, Nyanaponika and Hellmuth Hecker. *Great Disciples of the Buddha: Their Lives, Their Works, Their Legacy.* Somerville, Mass.: Wisdom Publications, 1997.

PERMISSIONS

Grateful acknowledgment is made to the following for permission to reprint previously published material:

© Buddhist Publication Society 1997. Reprinted from *Great Disciples of the Buddha: Their Lives, Their Works, Their Legacy* with permission of Wisdom Publications, 199 Elm St., Somerville, MA 02144, U.S.A., www.wisdompub.org.

From *Women in Early Buddhist Literature* by I. B. Horner by courtesy of the Buddhist Publication Society Inc., Sri Lanka.

Reprinted from *The First Buddhist Women: Translations and Commentary on the Terigatha* (1991) by Susan Murcott with permission of Parallax press, Berkeley, California.

From *Before He Was Buddha: The Life of Siddhartha* by Hammalawa Saddhatissa. Used by permission of Seastone.

From *Poems of the Early Buddhist Nuns* by C. A. F. Rhys Davids and K. R. Norman. Used by permission of the Pali Text Society.